BRIGHT NOTES

DARKNESS AT NOON AND THE AGE OF LONGING BY ARTHUR KOESTLER

Intelligent Education

Nashville, Tennessee

BRIGHT NOTES: Darkness at Noon and The Age of Longing
www.BrightNotes.com

No part of this publication may be used or reproduced in any manner whatsoever without written permission, except in the case of brief quotations in critical articles and reviews. For permissions, contact Influence Publishers http://www.influencepublishers.com.

ISBN: 978-1-645420-28-6 (Paperback)
ISBN: 978-1-645420-29-3 (eBook)

Published in accordance with the U.S. Copyright Office Orphan Works and Mass Digitization report of the register of copyrights, June 2015.

Originally published by Monarch Press.
William J. Fitzpatrick, 1966
2020 Edition published by Influence Publishers.

Interior design by Lapiz Digital Services. Cover Design by Thinkpen Designs.

Printed in the United States of America.

Library of Congress Cataloging-in-Publication Data forthcoming.
Names: Intelligent Education
Title: BRIGHT NOTES: Darkness at Noon and The Age of Longing
Subject: STU004000 STUDY AIDS / Book Notes

CONTENTS

1)	Introduction to Arthur Koestler	1
2)	Historical Background	13
3)	Introduction to Darkness At Noon	<OV>
4)	Textual Analysis	
	Part I - The First Hearing	37
	Part II - The Second Hearing	59
	Part III - The Third Hearing	68
	Part IV - The Grammatical Fiction	78
5)	Character Analyses	84
6)	General Commentary	100
7)	Essay Questions and Answers	111
8)	Textual Analysis	
	Part I	117
	Part II	126
9)	General Commentary	132

10)	Critical Commentary	145
11)	Essay Questions and Answers	149
12)	Bibliography	151

INTRODUCTION TO ARTHUR KOESTLER

INTRODUCTION

Arthur Koestler was born in Budapest, Hungary, in 1905. He is now living in England where he has devoted his recent years to writing about science and its implications for the humanities and for political and social and artistic life. He has told the story of his life in a four-volume autobiography: *Arrow in the Blue* and *The Invisible Writing* are a comprehensive account of his first thirty-five years of life; *Dialogue with Death* deals with the **episode** of his imprisonment by the Franco forces during the Spanish civil war; *Scum of the Earth* covers the years 1938-40, the time between Koestler's break with the Communist Party and his escape from occupied France to England; it is the period in which *Darkness at Noon* was written. In addition he relates the story of his conversion to, and turning from, Communism in a chapter in *The God that Failed*.

Koestler has always been very much a public man: he has always concerned himself with the great issues of the day; he has earned his livelihood in the field of journalism; he devoted seven years of his life to service in the largest and most aggressive mass movement of our time, Communism; his novels all have a contemporary historical significance; finally, his own life has a special public interest, and a reading of his autobiography in the five books mentioned above offers a rewarding discovery of important aspects of the history of the first half of the twentieth century.

CHILDHOOD

Koestler's parents were Jewish-his father, Hungarian, his mother, Austrian. Most of his relatives and in-laws were killed by the German National Socialists or the Communists. As his father was a well-to-do representative of English and German textile firms, Koestler had French and English governesses. At early age he knew French, German, English and Hungarian; later he learned a little Spanish and Russian. When World War I destroyed his father's business, the family moved to Vienna in 1915. His father's fortunes revived briefly in Vienna, but he again had to declare bankruptcy. The hyper-inflation which ruined the European middle class after World War I made it impossible for his father to reestablish himself. Koestler recalls his childhood as marked by loneliness, fear and guilt. Because of an early aptitude for engineering and science, Koestler was sent to secondary schools specializing in physics and engineering in Vienna and Budapest (1915-1921). From the age of seventeen to twenty (1922-24) Koestler studied at the polytechnic college of the University of Vienna.

ZIONISM

While a member of the Jewish burschenschaft (fraternity) at the university, Koestler discovered Zionism. Although his father had not been a conforming Jew and Koestler knew little of Judaism or the radical Zionist movement which wanted to establish a Jewish national state, he plunged eagerly into the social and political life of the Zionist group in the fraternity. (Koestler has had a sustained interest in Zionism but never in the religion of Judaism.) Shortly before he was to graduate from college and subsequently help support his family, Koestler burned his school records (which the students were supposed to maintain) and left for Palestine with the intention of working on a communal farm (1925-26). The reason for this impulsive action is not clear to Koestler even today. Apparently, the relatively conventional life of an engineer did not appeal to him; he needed something that could satisfy his idealistic longings. Finding that he was not cut out for life on a farm, young Koestler walked to Haifa and with a friend he set up a Zionist news service which had some initial success but failed after some months. For several months he barely managed to survive. He worked at odd jobs until finally, through an acquaintance, he got an opportunity to help edit a newspaper in Cairo. But this enterprise also failed after only three issues.

JOURNALISM

In the Spring of 1927 he went to Berlin to take a post with a splinter Zionist organization. Then, in September 1927 through a friend, he got a job as Middle East correspondent for the Ullstein newspapers, a huge and influential German publishing firm with headquarters in Berlin. He was now able to support his parents. After a couple of years as a well-paid newspaper correspondent living in Jerusalem and traveling around the Middle East-writing leisurely articles on random subjects, interviewing the great men of the area, instituting the Hebrew crossword puzzle - he transferred to the Paris office (June 1927). In 1929 his exclusive interview with the Nobel Prize winner Broglie, the French physicist, revealed his knowledge of science and he was sent to Berlin in 1930 as science editor of the most important of the Ullstein Berlin papers and science advisor of the Ullstein Trust. From the utter poverty of his early days in Palestine he had risen to an important and prestigious post as the chief interpreter of science for the readers of the papers of the Ullstein chain. In 1931 he became a foreign editor as well. At the age of 27 he was very successful and influential, with a career of great promise before him. He was the only correspondent on the arctic voyage of the Zeppelin in 1931. His articles were read by millions, and he even went on a lecture tour after the trip. But for the second time in his life he threw up a promising career for the sake of some idea (whatever other motivations there may have been).

COMMUNISM

As was the case for a great number of European intellectuals in quest of the absolute in the 1930's, Koestler discovered Marx and Lenin and Communism and the Communist Party. He became totally converted to the Communist ideology and joined the Party in 1931. Under orders he kept his important and useful post with the Ullstein firm. But he carelessly allowed a young man to report his pro-Communist activities to his superiors, and the firm gave Koestler a generous settlement and let him go in 1932. In July, 1932 Koestler was finally permitted to visit the "Promised Land" in order to write a book in praise of the Soviet Union - presumably for foreign consumption. Koestler spent the year 1932-33 in the U.S.S.R. and his account of that time is an example of how the eye sees what the mind tells it to. In retrospect he now realizes that the conditions under Communism were worse than under the former regime. During his stay in the Soviet Union he produced *Von Weissen Nachten und Roten Tagen (White Nights and Red Days)* which was published for the German minority living in the Ukraine. It was not published abroad, however.

By this time the Nazis had come to power in Germany and it was quite unsafe for Communists (and Koestler was both a Jew and a Communist). He was sent to Paris by the Comintern to work in the anti-Fascist propaganda campaign the exiled German Communist Party was conducting. From 1933 until 1938 Koestler held various jobs for the Communist Party (the Comintern-directed bureau for agitation and propaganda) in France. He helped to focus world attention on the German National Socialist regime and on the Fascists by working with a few others in an "institute for the study of Fascism" - actually, an agency of the Communist International directed by Moscow. He worked for the fabulous Willi Muenzenberg (Western European Propaganda Chief of the Comintern) who directed a worldwide propaganda network. But because he didn't want to be a paid Party worker Koestler left the Muenzenberg operation in 1934. At one point he attempted suicide because he was so depressed over the Party's criticism of a novel he wrote for "bourgeois subjectivity."

FIRST PUBLISHED WORKS

Between 1934 and 1939 he wrote (under a pseudonym) three "sex books." One of these, the *Encyclopedia of Sexual Knowledge*, became an international bestseller. Between 1935 and 1938 he worked on his first published novel, *The Gladiators*, while living in Paris, Zurich and Budapest. He also translated a propaganda novel into German for Muenzenberg and worked for a Communist Front press service in Zurich.

PROPAGANDA TRAVELS

He became part of the largely successful effort of the Communists to get the world to accept their version of the

Spanish civil war. In August 1936 he posed as a right-wing Hungarian newspaper man (he was also accredited to a British paper) and visited Franco's headquarters for the Communist propaganda apparatus. After a narrow escape he worked in London as a liaison with the English Communists. He returned to Spain in 1936 (this time on the anti-Franco side of the front) and then to Paris where he wrote a propaganda book on the Spanish civil war for the Communists. He later admitted that it included unverified charges. (The book was published in France as *L'Espagne Ensanglante*.) He again returned to Spain in early 1937 and was soon arrested. He spent about a hundred days in prison - from February 9 to May 14, 1937.

BREAK WITH COMMUNISM

The days Koestler spent in the Spanish prison were a turning point in his life. He had what would have to be called a mystical experience. He did not recount it in *Dialogue with Death*, the book which related his Spanish prison **episode**, because he had not fully come to terms with what he calls in *The Invisible Writing* "the hours by the window." In his cell he achieved what he describes as the tranquility of understanding. He perceived the basic truths of human solidarity. The "I" was dissolved in the whole. He came to see (implicitly) that the abstractions of Communist ideology - "Mankind," "History" - were unreal. Thus, his sense of responsibility in human society was enhanced and deepened while the hold that Communist ideology had on him was mortally weakened. The concrete effects of his experience were delayed, but Koestler derives his break with the Communist Party and his later hostility to its aggression from the spiritual transformation he felt in the Spanish prison.

MYSTICISM

Koestler's writings, fiction and non-fiction, took on a mystical, "spiritual" dimension. He accorded a respectability and validity to what Freud calls the "oceanic sense," to intimations of another order of "reality," another "logic," an "invisible writing" which we ignore at our peril. This is as far as Koestler will go in granting the validity of religious insights. But many consider that this dimension has given to his writing a depth and relevance which keeps it above the trivial.

ANTI-COMMUNIST; ANTI-NAZI

When he finished *Dialogue with Death* in the autumn of 1937, he was sent to Greece, Palestine and Egypt as a correspondent for an English newspaper. In early 1938 he lectured in England for the Left Book Club. He revealed his break from the Communist Party by refusing to follow the Party Line in a speech he gave in Paris in the Spring of 1938. In July 1938 he finished *The Gladiators* which deals with the abortive Roman slave rebellion led by Spartacus in the first century A.D. From 1938 to 1940 he worked on *Darkness at Noon*, inspired by the Moscow Trials which had just come to a conclusion. For a time in 1938 he was the editor of the anti-Nazi/anti-Communist German exile paper Die Zukunft. Before the hostilities with the Germans began, the French kept a close watch on all Germans - especially German Communists. His room was searched by the police several times. After the French declared war on Germany in October 1939, he was arrested and spent four months (October to January) in a French concentration camp. Just before the Germans occupied France, he was arrested again but managed to escape. As a Jew with a Communist past he might well have been killed had he been caught by the advancing Nazis. He managed to escape that fate by joining the French Foreign Legion. He then made his way to Marseilles, thence to North Africa, Lisbon, and, finally, to interment in a jail in London.

BACKGROUND OF WORKS

He saw *Darkness at Noon* through the press while still in prison. Before he joined the Army he published *Scum of the Earth*. This was his first book in English. *Arrival and Departure*, his first novel written in English, was published in 1943. During the war he wrote a number of essays for journals and newspapers in England and the United States. These were collected in *The Yogi and the Commissar* (1945), and were the first series of Koestler's post-Party examination of the world he lived in. A second collection of public essays was published in 1955 (*The Trail of the Dinosaur*). After *The Age of Longing* (completed 1950), Koestler set to work on his two-volume autobiography *Arrow in the Blue* (1952) and *The Invisible Writing*. The sensational international success of *Darkness at Noon* after the Second World War and the originality and shrewdness of his essays, enabled him to travel widely. He finally settled down permanently in England in 1952. Since 1955, he has devoted his time to writing about science.

Koestler's work may be divided into four classes: autobiography; novels; political and social essays; science. The first three are intimately connected and illumine each other. The last represents a return to his interest in understanding the natural laws which are written in "the invisible writing."

AUTOBIOGRAPHY

Koestler's autobiography (in five books) has three chief interests: it is marvelously informative on the subject of Communism; it is a first-rate job of reporting on a number of other important aspects of life in the first half of the twentieth century; it is, in Koestler's own words, a detailed case history of an intellectual whose life story helps to explain the political and social history of our age.

Dialogue with Death, based on his prison diaries and recounting the experiences of his last trip to Spain was written and published later that year. (*Dialogue with Death* was first published in England along with a good deal of *L'Espagne Ensanglante'* as Spanish Testament. However, *Dialogue with Death* is available separately, in a paperback edition.) Scum of the Earth was an account of Koestler's years in France from 1938 to 1940. *The God That Failed* consists of six authors' comments on their disenchantment with Communism.

The Arrow in the Blue and *The Invisible Writing* help one to understand what it meant to be a Communist in the 1930's. In addition Koestler offers his own analysis of why people become Communists. His discussion of the Moscow Trials, the Spanish civil war, and of many other details of Party propaganda and Party life, as well as the record of his own activities in the period, make an illuminating and vivid contribution to the history of the Communist movement. After reading Koestler's accounts, one can have no doubt of the character of Communism as a "faith." And the picture of the impotence of Europe in the face of the rise of Communism and Fascism is still instructive in the mid-sixties.

NOVELS

Each of Koestler's five novels is part of what Orwell said was his attempt "to write contemporary history, but unofficial history, the kind that is ignored in the textbooks and lied about in the newspapers." *The Gladiators* (1939), a novel about the slave rebellion against Rome in the first century, deals with the corrupting influence of power and with the "psychology of the masses." Some critics have called it Koestler's best novel. *Darkness at Noon* (1940) - Koestler's generally acknowledged masterpiece - is based on the Moscow Purge Trials of the thirties. A good account of these trials is given in Koestler's *The Invisible Writing*. *Arrival and Departure* (1943 - Kaestler's first novel in English) is the story of a Communist intellectual who is led to the conclusion (by psychoanalysis) that his revolutionary activities derive from neurotic motives. Koestler attempts to demonstrate that ethical imperatives cannot be analyzed away or rationalized by science. *Thieves in the Night* (1946) deals with the attempt to establish a Jewish nation in Palestine. The questions of Jewish-Arab relations, Zionism, terrorism, and Great Britain's involvement are analyzed in a novel which seems to plead the Zionist cause and even to justify terrorism (the latter is interesting in view of Koestler's treatment of the ends-and-means **theme** in *Darkness at Noon*). *The Age of Longing* (1951) presents the author's view of the underlying malaise of the mid-century as manifested in the West's confusion in the Cold War.

There seems to be a general agreement that most of Koestler's novels are excessively "skeletel" in structure (V.S. Prichett). And they seem so tied to external historical events that they appear to lack that plot structure, characterization, and fictionalized integration, which readers of the English novel have come to expect. It is therefore a mistake not to approach them as "novels of ideas." So read they can be very satisfying as dramatic transcriptions or intellectual problems and arguments about historical events. But *Darkness at Noon* will satisfy virtually all novelistic criteria.

ESSAYS

The Yogi and the Commissar (1945) and *The Trail of the Dinosaur* (1955) include Koestler's writings on public and political subjects in the fifteen years after his arrival in England. Of his political writings one can say that he has consistently avoided the kind of selective indignation described by George Orwell: "The sin of nearly all left-wingers from 1933 onwards is that they have wanted to be anti-Fascist without being anti-totalitarian." Koestler has continually incurred the wrath of the Left by his many essays showing the deceit and tyranny of Communism and exposing the myth of the Soviet Union. His essays treat most of the **themes** that appear in his novels and are useful for anyone studying them. Promise and Fulfillment (1950) is a discursive companion to Thieves in the Night. The book deals with the history and nature of the Zionist attempt to set up a Jewish national state in Palestine. Koestler concludes by suggesting that Jews should either emigrate to Israel or abandon Judaism to merge into the culture of the country in which they reside. *The Lotus and the Robot* (1961) recounts Koestler's investigation of the "contemplative" cultures of India and Japan. He concludes that the East has little to offer Western civilization. Reflections on Hanging is a criticism of capital punishment in England.

SCIENCE

One of the **themes** that runs through the two collections of essays is the problem of making a new synthesis of faith and reason (cf. *The Age of Longing*). Koestler's three books on science are motivated at least remotely by this same idea. *Insight and Outlook* (1949) is a preliminary attempt at an integration of science, art and ethics. *The Sleepwalkers* (1959) is a history of cosmology, especially as seen in the work of the great astronomers. The book offers new and exciting material on Galileo and Kepler. *The Act of Creation* (1964) is a study of the psychology of creativity in the arts and sciences. On this last work, one is tempted to quote Koestler against himself: "When my writing has run dry, I shall sit for eight hours at my desk, growing piles over some boring and meritorious piece of research, as an atonement for an unknown original sin." (*Arrow in the Blue*)

Although Koestler's speculation on the possibility of achieving a new synthesis of science and the "oceanic feeling" for the purpose of reintegrating the Western mind seems relevant but superficial, it is probably safe to say that *The Sleepwalkers* will retain a place in the literature of the history of cosmology. His autobiography will retain a place as a significant case history in the records of the history of this century (especially of Communism); and it is likely that *Darkness at Noon* will have a permanent, if minor, place in the novelistic record of the perversions of the mind through ideology and as a classic study of the Communist mind.

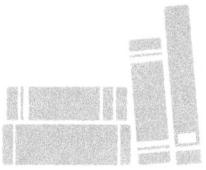

DARKNESS AT NOON

HISTORICAL BACKGROUND

INTRODUCTION

It cannot be denied that the chief interest in *Darkness at Noon* is its treatment of historical events. At least, what draws readers to the book, if not what holds them and brings them back, is its fidelity to certain sensational events of recent history and to a strange phenomenon which is shaking our century. The novel is historical in two senses: 1) it presents, in imaginative and dramatic but largely accurate form, a complex of incidents relating to what has become one of the causes célébres of twentieth-century politics - the Great Purge of the Communist Party of the Soviet Union in the 1930's; 2) in the portrayal of its chief character, Rubashov, the novel is a revelation of the Communist mind, a mind so alien to the tradition of Western society that it is largely incomprehensible. The novel's inevitable appeal is compounded because the phenomenon of Communism - the Communist Party and the Communist mind - exists and is relevant to the reader today, and it will remain so tomorrow.

It must be emphasized that although Koestler speaks of the "German dictatorship," a "Belgian port," the "French police," "the

Party," the "Central Committee," "the Dialectic," and the like, he nowhere uses the term "Communist" or "Communism," nor does he mention the U.S.S.R. or name Stalin or Lenin. It is likely that because the reader would be aware of historical references and allusions, the author wished to protect the novel against the appearances of propaganda, of political pamphleteering, by avoiding terms so charged with emotion. It may be also that the use of certain proper names, especially of persons living at the time of publication, would have given the novel a journalistic coarseness, which might have inhibited the reader's recognition of the free, imaginative, universal - novelistic - life of the book. Furthermore, it is entirely possible to understand the novel without any thought of the history to which it refers. This is the proof that *Darkness at Noon* is a successful work of creative fiction: a revelation of essential human experience. Nevertheless, the novel is most intimately involved with some extremely important events of twentieth-century history, and the reader who is unaware of the context will not be able to adequately appreciate Koestler's effort.

The specific historical events in the novel all belong to the history of the Communist Party. And the **climax** of this history, the central event of the novel - indeed, the event that provoked the novel and which the novel was written to explain - is the Great Purge which Stalin carried out systematically and ruthlessly from about 1934 to 1939.

THE GREAT PURGE

In *The God that Failed* (see Bibliography) Koestler and several other distinguished writers describe how they became either Communists or Communist sympathizers. Those six writers represent the thousands who saw in Communism and in the

Soviet Union secular salvation for a suffering humanity. Many had turned a blind eye on the dismal social existence that followed the Bolshevik coup d'etat in 1917. But then the Purge began in 1935, these Communists and sympathizers were faced with an inevitable crisis of faith. They had either to reaffirm, in the knowledge of the fantastic terror of Stalin and the Soviet Union, their devotion to Communism, or else to accuse the Party of despotism, betrayal, corruption, deceit and contradiction. The choice was unavoidable because the Party was now killing its own. Those accused of sabotage and treason - of being British or German agents! - (Zinoviev, Krestinsky, Bukharin, Kamenev, Radek, Piatkov, Rakovsky, Krylenko, Rykov, Yagoda, Smyrnov, Mrachkovsky, Tuchachvesky, and thousands of lesser lights) were some of the greatest names in the Communist Party of the Soviet Union. In the words of Whittaker Chambers, "they were the Communist Party." Zinoviev was president of the Communist International. After he was shot, Bukharin, a noted author and Communist theoretician, veteran of the October Revolution (1917), former editor of Pravda, succeeded him as president of the International. Bukharin was an important member of the Party before Stalin achieved his prominence. Yagoda was head of the Secret Police. Mrachkovsky had been a famous general in the Civil War. All had important positions in the Soviet Communist Party or the Soviet State. Their service to Communism, before it gained control of the Russian Empire and after, was legendary. During the Purge these heroes of the October Revolution were accused of the worst possible crime: trying, in various ways, to destroy the work of the Revolution - that is, trying to undo their own work! Thousands were shot, imprisoned and executed. Estimates of the number killed in the years of the Great Purge vary from the hundreds of thousands to the millions.

The Party faithful were faced with a shocking dilemma: either the Party, hitherto a stunning success, was rotten to the core, its leaders incredible frauds; or they were innocent and the Party was now in the grip of a terrible despot who would ruin it. The trauma of the event was heightened by the fact that many of the accused confessed their crimes in the most abject and shameless way in a series of "show trials" that Stalin arranged in order to justify to the population of the Soviet Union as well as to the world at large, the brutal repression of the Party's rule and the failure of its policies. The fact that the Purge was the conclusion of a struggle for control of the Communist Party (this meant every national Communist Party including the Communist Party of the United States had its own purge directed from Moscow) between "Stalinists" and various "oppositions" did not answer me disturbing questions the Purge raised. Why did Stalin, even if he was right in his policies, have to kill so many valiant champions of Communism? Why did he have to accuse them of the utterly incredible charges of treason add sabotage - that is, of anti-Communist activities? Finally, why did so many confess to these accusations?

As a result of the Purge many left the Party for good, and of these, many became enemies of Communism. For many, even today, the Purge is the chief blot on the Communist record. And Stalin's ruthless destruction of his adversaries (and potential adversaries!) focused the world's attention on the deviousness and abomination of the Communist Party's methods. Even after the period of the Purges and Stalin's death, Communism's total disregard of ethical restraints in dealing with people who get in the way of a policy or program remains a continuing indictment of the Party wherever it may be found.

Further, recognition of the despotism within the Communist Party made it more difficult for Party members to rationalize the thorough repression of virtually all political and social freedoms in the Soviet Union: it was no longer possible to say that "the Party had its reasons," when the Party itself was either corrupt or governed by the most absolute and brutal of dictatorships.

Most Party members accommodated themselves to the Great Purge. Some sympathizers, no doubt, did so out of ignorance or naiveté, some Party members out of practical convenience. But these people are not interesting. What of the orthodox Communists who looked the truth in the face and yet kept their faith? What, in fact, of those whom Koestler calls the "hard core," whose record of fearless and selfless devotion to principle made it impossible to explain their confessions of "counterrevolutionary crimes" as the result of torture, fear, or the protection of hostages? *Darkness at Noon* is the attempt to present in the form of a novel: 1) the impact of the Great Purge on the faithful of the Party (e.g., Rubashov's reactions to Stalin's execution of the men in the photograph); 2) the arrest, imprisonment and trial of such a hero of the Communist Revolution; 3) the process by which Stalin's tyranny in the U.S.S.R., his killing off of the "oppositionists," and his extreme defamation of them in show trials were rationalized by the Party faithful (e.g., Rubashov's theory of "relative maturity of the masses"); 4) the way in which the "hard core" brought themselves to confess to the false and absurd (Part III). The book thus renders intelligible the Great Purge, and thereby explains how the ideology of Communism (as opposed to the Great Power, the Soviet Union) could have survived what might well have been a finishing blow.

THE FAILURE OF COMMUNISM IN THE U.S.S.R.

The reader will recall that the Belgian dockworkers inquired about the Soviet Union "like children asking the exact size of the grapes in Canaan." Koestler used the Biblical term "promised land" to convey the hope the U.S.S.R. would symbolize. And it was not only to members of the Party that the homeland of Communism was a socialist Utopia. Party propaganda had convinced many non-Communists that the Soviet Union was solving the social and economic problems of Western Society. But the reality of the Soviet State included widespread famine, millions in Siberian concentration camps, capital punishment for trivial offenses, a sub-Czarist standard of living, persecution of religions and the national minority groups, corruption, apathy, cynicism: in short, a brutal dictatorship worse than any Czarist regime. Like the Purge, the dismal failure of the Soviet Union to live up to promise and report - in economic and social achievements and in political and cultural liberties - was a shock to much of the world, and many Party members. It was another test of faith. And though it was easier to rationalize than the Purge, yet it had to be explained, it had to disturb - at least momentarily - sensitive and informed "comrades." *Darkness At Noon* dramatizes some of the political repression (in the treatment and histories of the various prisoners) and the distorted personal relationships the regime creates (e.g., Wassilij and his daughter). It relates (indirectly, through the conversations between Rubashov and Ivanov and in Rubashov's meditations) the other failures of the U.S.S.R. And it shows how the Party hard core explained and justified the terror without losing their Communist faith (e.g., Ivanov's rebuttal at the end of Part II, Rubashov's theory, Gletkin's speeches in Part III, Chapter IV).

Of course, both the Purge and conditions in the Soviet Union redounded to the detriment of Stalin, who, as No. 1, is characterized as a self-glorifying and ruthless despot. (For Stalin and Lenin, see Character Analysis.)

THE COMINTERN

Darkness at Noon reveals the Communist Party in action, not only in the U.S.S.R., in the dictatorship of Stalin, and the Great Purge, but in its dealings with the Party faithful abroad during the thirties. The sacrifice of loyal Party members and innocent bystanders (the men in the photograph and Arlova) reached into other national Parties. These were not autonomous political groups functioning in the traditional life of a nation, but parts of an integrated international movement with headquarters in Moscow.

The Communist International (or Comintern, or Third International) was founded by Lenin for the purpose of coordinating and controlling the Communist movement around the world.

All the orthodox Communist parties joined the Comintern by subscribing to the rules set down by the Moscow headquarters which determined organization, Party Line and tactics, and specific activities of the various national parties. All parties had to defend the Soviet Union and support its foreign policy. The non-Russian Communist parties were bound and subservient to the U.S.S.R. for three reasons: 1) a common ideology or faith; 2) the foreign groups, despised and harassed in their own countries, were dependent on the U.S.S.R. for material, financial, and moral support; 3) the U.S.S.R. was the only place where Communism controlled territory and non-Communist populations; it was therefore invested with enormous prestige: Communism was coming into being there. The parties belonging to the International were admonished to conduct periodic "purges" of alien elements. These "purges" have characterized Communist parties to this day.

One of the functions of the flashbacks is to extend the action of the novel beyond the borders of the Soviet Union and thereby present a fuller picture of the Party's universal treachery and deceit. Thus, Rubashov, a member of the Central Committee of the Communist Party of the Soviet Union, gives orders to members of the Belgian and the German parties. The point that emerges from the betrayal of Richard to the Gestapo and the thankless exploitation of the Belgian dockworkers is the total disregard for human feelings, individual rights or past record of service to the Party. Any member is only a tool for use or disposal as the Party sees fit. This is what disturbs Rubashov's faith, what drives Richard to rebellion and Loewy to suicide. And these are not "capitalists," "exploiters" or "counterrevolutionaries," but the Party's faithful flock.

It is not that the Party is without principle: it is ruthlessly consistent to the principle of survival and self-aggrandizement so that it can strengthen and spread Communism. But this principle appears to require the Party to persecute its own, to lie to its own, to justify any expedient that will prevent a material loss to it. Honor means success. The foreign policy of the Soviet Union (the one place where the Party had full control of a society) will sacrifice foreign Communists to its enemies in order to guarantee its security. The Party can be trusted by no one, not even its members.

Koestler's treatment of Party history in the thirties also reveals the essentials dogma which defined and justified the Party (then as now): the Party is a militant secular church, claiming that the will of "History" commands it to destroy present human society and make a new one. Thus *Darkness at Noon* reveals the nature of Communism - the faith, the creed, the ideology, the mass movement - the nature of the phenomenon which was and remains so important a feature of social reality in the twentieth century. This is the purpose of all of Rubashov's meditations on the nature of the Party, on the "laws of History," on the "Dialectic of History" (History, as an idea to be worshipped, is capitalized in order to distinguish it from the history that everyone lives).

THE OPPOSITION

There was indeed an "opposition" to Stalin, as portrayed in the novel. But as Rubashov notes, it was not the slightest match for Stalin's determined drive. The opposition to Stalin was a struggle for power carried out without scruple. But the personal struggle for power, as is inevitable in the Party, was conducted in ideological terms - that is, as a disagreement over what was the correct "Party Line." It is unnecessary for the reader to know all the subtleties of Stalin's struggle with various "oppositionists." Koestler makes three points about the opposition as represented by Rubashov, old Kieffer, and the unnamed "men in the photograph": 1) they were ineffectual, vacillating, and weak in their opposition; 2) some were prompted by considerations that one might call "humanitarian" (disturbed by the lack of democracy in the Party, the harshness of Party retribution against its own, and its despotism and failure in the U.S.S.R.); 3) Rubashov apparently has been a "Trotskyist."

Two or three times in the novel Koestler has Gletkin refer to the partisans of immediate aid to other Communist parties in order to spread revolution, who therefore opposed No. 1's policy of consolidating and protecting the "Bastion of the Revolution." Thus, for purposes of economy, Koestler reduces the opponents of Stalin on Party policy to the "Trotskyists" - though, to be sure, Koestler never mentions Trotsky's name. Leon Trotsky was one of the great figures of the Communist movement, a mighty theorist, a principal organizer of the October 1917 Revolution which brought the Bolsheviks to power, the Commissar of War largely responsible for the defeat of the "White" forces in the civil war that followed the Revolution. His doctrine of immediately spreading the revolution around the world clashed with the Stalinist line of "socialism in one country [U.S.S.R.]" until the Soviet Union was powerful and secure. Although he was exiled by Stalin in 1929, the "Moscow Trials" charged the defendants with being part of a plot against Stalin's life engineered by Trotsky. (Stalin had Trotsky assassinated by an agent in 1940.) Thus, Gletkin tells Rubashov that he was one of the "adventurers" who would risk" what we had won to promote the revolution abroad."

THE REVOLUTION AND THE CIVIL WAR

The "Revolution" which is continually referred to in the book means either the October 1917 Bolshevik coup which brought the Communist Party to power in the former Russian Empire, or the on-going fulfillment of the aims of that Revolution in the U.S.S.R. under the guidance of the Party and Stalin. The Revolution was a coup d'etat which the Bolsheviks (Communists) carried out against the Mensheviks (Democratic Socialists who controlled the government after the February 1917 Revolution toppled the Czarist regime). From 1918 to 1920 a savage civil war was fought between the Red (Communist) and White (all varieties of anti-Communist, including socialist and Czarist) Russians. Rubashov was a daring commander in the Red Army which saved the Revolution. So were many of the "oppositionists."

The term "counterrevolutionary" means simply "anti-Communist" - opposed to the spirit or detail of the fruit of Party action, hence resisting or opposing the Party (i.e., the course of "History").

GERMANY; ITALY; HUNGARY

The other significant events which enter *Darkness at Noon* are: the advent of the German National Socialist Workers party (Nazi) regime in Germany in 1993 and the consequent destruction of the German Communist party; the Fascist regime under Mussolini in Italy which began its subjugation of Ethiopia in 1935; the brief Communist regime under Bela Kun (later murdered by Stalin) in Hungary (1919). It was Koestler's intention to suggest a parallel between the German National Socialist and the Soviet dictatorships, a point which has become commonplace now, but which was practically unheard of and took a certain courage in 1938-40, when Koestler wrote *Darkness at Noon*. In his book on Koestler, John Atkins [see Bibliography] points out that Soviet troops in Sinkiang (in China) were doing substantially the same thing in 1934 for which the world was to condemn Mussolini in 1935. When 406 (a veteran of the Hungarian Commune) introduces the anthem of the Communist movement, the incident dramatizes the terrible ironic contrast between Communism's promise and its fulfillment.

HISTORY OMITTED

There are two events missing from this historical novel which we might expect to find in it. One is the treaty (1939) between National Socialist Germany and the Soviet Union, which provided for the partition of Poland and the Baltic States and which secured Hitler's rear as he attacked France and the Low Countries. This complicity in aggression with its so-called archenemy - even more than the Great Purge - opened the eyes of many to Communism's policy of utter expediency which would sacrifice anything for practical advantage. And no one could fault Stalin for being inconsistent: the Pact was perfectly good

Communist strategy. Another reversal of the party line was the change in 1935 from a policy of aggressive political combat with all non-Communist groups (e.g., Socialists were called "Social Fascists") to active collaboration, with a view to gaining power in coalition governments, with all leftist and liberal groups who were opposed to Communism's conscious enemies. This tactic was called the "Popular Front." It lasted from 1935 to the Nazi-Communist pact in 1939. Koestler is silent about these two proofs of Communist expediency and treachery. But his silence is artful, because the infamous events are present in the reader's mind and provide ironic comment on Richard's protest to Rubashov (shortly before he turns him over to the Gestapo) and on the accusation that Rubashov conspired to deal with the Germans in order to overthrow No. 1.

SUBSEQUENT HISTORY

Events subsequent to the writing of *Darkness at Noon* have spectacularly confirmed Koestler's hypothesis. In 1956, at the Twentieth Congress of the Communist Party of the Soviet Union, Premier Nikita Khrushchev attacked Stalin, who had died in 1953, and declared the defendants of the Moscow trials innocent of the specific charges (treason, assassination, sabotage) brought against them (thus fulfilling the promise Gletkin made Rubashov!). (Khrushchev then undertook a purge of his own opposition!) In *The Invisible Writing* Koestler tells how when his former close associate in the Party, Otto Katz, was being charged for treason in the purge trials in Czechoslovakia in 1952, he paraphrased Rubashov's confession (itself a paraphrase of Bukharin's) in order to let the world know that the same process described by his former friend Koestler in *Darkness at Noon* was at work in his case. (Though whether he borrowed Rubashov's speech to indicate the insincerity of his confession or ironically to affirm his persisting faith cannot be certain.) And in his fine introduction to the Signet paperback edition of *Darkness at Noon*, Peter Viereck relates how the same reasoning Ivanov and Gletkin used on Rubashov caused a prominent Hungarian Bolshevik to go to his death confessing to the false charge of treason. A number of books have served subsequently to confirm, both in principle and in detail, Koestler's notion of how the brave old Bolsheviks came to confess so meekly to Stalin's trumped-up charges. Of these, the most authoritative is by General Walter Krivitsky (once of the Soviet Military Intelligence, assassinated by the Soviet Secret Police in Washington, D.C.) in his book *I Was Stalin's Agent*. He tells how Mrachkovsky and Smirnov were brought to confess by appeal to Communist logic. (It would appear from Krivitsky's account that they confessed in order to strengthen the Party, after having lost the power struggle; while Rubashov confesses because he concludes that Stalin has been right in his policies all along. But the slight difference in reasoning is unimportant beside the same selfless faith in, and devotion to, the Party which both writers see as the motive for embracing and aiding their murderer.)

Thus, Koestler's novel is historically accurate; he has delineated the nature of the faith which moves the hard core Communists wherever and whenever they are to be found.

THE COMMUNIST MIND

This phrase could serve as a proper subtitle of *Darkness at Noon*. This is the historical phenomenon - the contemporary phenomenon - which subsumes all the other **themes** of the novel. The novel is a portrait, a representation, of the Communist mind. In Rubashov we find out - at least with an insight rare in writings on the subject - what this mind is, by what logic it functions, by what faith it lives, why it can create and believe a "truth" the ordinary mind finds incredible and absurd. *Darkness at Noon* is one of four books cited by Frank Meyer, in his classic scholarly study of the subject, as best revealing the "subjective aspect" of the Communist movement. The distinguishing features of this mind - what permits it lovingly to do service for its executioner as it goes to its death - is its utter submission to the "Dialectic of History," in whose purpose and end it believes itself to be participating.

The Communist believes that the "laws of History have been revealed by Lenin and Marx. The course of history has been the dynamic unfolding of man in society through his transformation of nature. Succeeding socio-economic systems proceed according to a "dialectical" law, where one social form opposes or negates another to produce a third "higher" form. This process continues, in the detail of events as well as in larger historical units, until all "negative" elements in society preventing the full realization of human nature have themselves been "negated." The perfection of man and human society is the culmination of this historical process, the realization of Communism, a state of perfection which is the end of "History," a Utopia peopled by a super-humanity. To the Communist this earthly heaven represents a version of what Christians call "salvation." It draws from the dedicated hard core of the Party the same zeal and devotion that unity with God in eternity causes in the Christian saint. (But whereas sanctity for the Christian means conforming to the will of God, for the Communist it consists in conforming to the concrete requirements of the "Dialectic," of the historical process leading inexorably to Communism.) However, "History" has ordained that the unsophisticated masses of workers who are to overthrow "capitalist" society must have the guidance of a "vanguard" - the Communist Party, whose members think and act together to express the will of "History." The emergence of the Party coincides, in general, with the decadence of "capitalism." The Party must promote world revolution to bring about socialism, the "negative" of the "alien" existence of capitalism. What follows this opposition of "antithesis" to "thesis" is the "synthesis" of a "friendly", "truly human" existence: the Communist paradise.

In his valuable chapter on *Darkness at Noon* in *The Invisible Writing* Koestler acknowledges that Rubashov is modeled on Trotsky, Bukharin and Radek, both in his personality and his physical appearance. Rubashov's declaration at the trial follows that of Bukharin. Rubashov's own mental struggle is Koestler's answer to the question, "Why did Bukharin and the others confess to the ridiculous accusations of the Moscow trials?" They confessed, the author tells us, because they were convinced that it was "logical" to do so, that it made sense, that it would be "sentimental," "bourgeois," "counterrevolutionary" and stupid to do otherwise. A refusal to do so would be an irrational betrayal of the faith without which they were nothing. They had been wrong in their "opposition," their thinking had run counter to the "Dialectic of History", and the only way they could repair the damage they might have done the Party was by undertaking this one last assignment. This is what we learn from Rubashov's ratiocination. Bogrov died in silence - no doubt there were many such deaths during the Purge - but, in so doing, the final movement of his life was against the stream of "History." Rubashov, Bukharin and the others, Koestler claims, needed "to die in the state of grace" (to borrow the Christian formulation of a happy death). The people who labor for the Party - the hard core who run the machine - are driven by just such a profound faith, just such a worshipping desire and need to advance the correct Party Line. Symptoms of the kind of anxiety the Christian feels at the thought of "losing his soul" or his faith or being excommunicated from the Church can be seen in Rubashov's "crisis of faith."

This is how Koestler makes sense of the Communist mind, of the phenomenon that has puzzled so many non-Communists to the point where they deny that it exists: Communists (Koestler says) actually believe the ideology they talk of incessantly among themselves. Many persons resisted Koestler's analysis when it was published; they explained the confessions exclusively by torture, drug and blackmail. Koestler acknowledged6 that these methods worked on some. But as far as the fearless old Bolsheviks are concerned, only Koestler's explanation is compatible with the actions of both the winners and the losers in the Purge; for both behaved unintelligibly by any ordinary logic. Further, Koestler's analysis explains more than the Purge: it presents the only principle which makes sense of the whole Communist enterprise - so alien to Western rationality. It is therefore a mistake for the reader to focus exclusively on the Moscow trials and the Purge. The confessions of Bukharin, Mrachkovsky, Smirnov and the will to turn the U.S.S.R. into a house of terror and the declaration of war against the entire non-Communist world and the sacrifice of German Party members to the Gestapo and the sacrifice of Poles to Communism's archenemy Hitler and the desecration of the memories of the men who created the Communist State and the destruction of millions of human beings and the stern discipline of a religious order stretching across national boundaries and environmental backgrounds - all these things together - for only an explanation covering all of the Party's activities can render it intelligible - can be explained only by taking the ideology of Communism seriously, by assuming that Communists do, in fact, believe that they have discovered the "laws of History"; that they can fulfill themselves only by helping to bring into being that transformation of man and society which is the goal of historical development. It should be clear now that *Darkness at*

Noon envelops a much larger historical context than the famous trials which occasioned its writing.

The nonrational, demonic faith exhibited in Rubashov, Gletkin, Ivanov and 406 therefore explains the success of Communist license - the freedom from the accumulated ethical restraints of Western civilization - which is the scandal of the rest of the world and which provokes Rubashov to question and almost to renounce the Party's authority. Because the Party is the expressive form of "History's" intent, because it points the way to earthly salvation, because salvation is at stake - mundane, routine, political events are charged with an apocalyptic significance. Any "objectively wrong" act can be regarded as sacrilegious and blasphemous, and takes its quality from the apocalyptic context of the Party's revolutionary activity as the midwife of "History." This apocalyptic mentality flows immediately from the content of Communist ideology possessing the minds of the Party hard core, and results inevitably in the license which permits No. 1 to use the murder and deceit of the Moscow Trials in order to control the "masses." The apocalyptic mentality is most clearly seen in the justification (by Ivanov and, later, Rubashov) given for No. 1's policy: in view of its Communist rule, the U.S.S.R. - the "Bastion" of the Revolution, covering one-sixth of the land surface of the earth - participates in "History"; it is contemporary testimony to the truth of Communism; therefore it must be protected with monumental caution and ruthless organization. The Communist has a fearful responsibility: who is Rubashov to criticize No. 1 - he would probably be just as "consequent" if the Party's leadership were his.

If one rejects Koestler's assumption that Communist ideology is believed literally, then one is likely to be faced with a dilemma: either to accept that the fantastic reality of Communist activities is not intelligible, or to ignore much of the reality so that it will yield to analysis. Koestler's common-sense acceptance (based on his own experience in the Party) permits him to see the unity and consistency in the maze of the Communist movement.

KOESTLER'S CRITIQUE OF COMMUNISM

As the foregoing analysis indicates, *Darkness at Noon* is an historical novel not only because it reenacts history, but also because it is about history; it comments on the events it presents. And Koestler is not merely offering an hypothesis on the motive for certain of the confessions of the Moscow Trials. He wishes to transcend the individual tragedy of Rubashov's failure to break through the prison of ideology and suggest to the reader what is wrong with the faith for which the old Bolsheviks and the new are willing to murder and to die.

The book is first of all addressed to English readers, and secondly to European (non-Communist) readers. It therefore assumes the context of their ethical assumptions, which are the product, more or less, of the Christian tradition. This juxtaposition of Communist deeds and the traditional ethical precepts solicits a general condemnation from the reader. The author need merely inform him, dramatically, about the subject; the ethical judgment follows.

The author's destructive critique takes several lines:

1) Rubashov enumerates the various counts of tyranny and suffering which characterize the rule of the Communist party in the "Homeland of the Revolution."

2) Gletkin's reminiscences and the story of Rubashov's past - including the stories of Richard, Arlova and Little

Loewy - dramatize the annihilation of the individual in the international Communist movement.

3) Rubashov's fate at the hands of the Party, and that of 406, 402, Harelip, Ivanov, the Peasant and the others, confirm, as it were, the impressions the reader gets from the flashbacks.

4) Rubashov's interior struggle ends in a willful (though only partially successful) suppression of what Christians would regard as the most "human" aspect of the man: the stirrings of charity and guilt in him, the "natural" impulses which are of a piece with conventional ethics and which cause him to question his Party faith. The fact that Communism requires such a suppression and can successfully achieve it in a man like Rubashov is an even more damaging indictment of the "philosophy" of Communism than the suffering it causes (see points 1, 2 and 3). This is why more time is given to dramatizing this thesis than to the lack of political, social and economic freedom in the U.S.S.R.

5) The profoundest observation Koestler makes on the phenomenon of Communism does not fully emerge until Part IV (though the careful reader will spot it earlier). Here Koestler suggests that the defects of Communism are not due to the appearance of a Stalin. Rather, as Koestler indicates in *The Invisible Writing*, "the seeds of corruption had already been present in the work of Marx" (p. 26). The crucial flaw lay in thinking that there are "laws of History" - history in its fullness, past, present and future - which are accessible to human reason. The Communists are driven to know all; this knowledge, they believe, gives them the license to do all in order to transform man and society. ("We are tearing the old skin off mankind and giving it a new one," says Ivanov.) Koestler wishes, then, to connect the distortions of human behavior which are the norm

in the Communist Party with the original speculation on the meaning of history that gave (and gives) birth to the Communist Revolution. Thus, it cannot be said that Koestler is only pointing at the "degradation of the Revolution," the "betrayal of the Revolution": the "cash value" (to borrow an expression of Eliseo Vivas's) of the Revolution and of the grandiose abstractions of Communist ideology is the execution cellar, the concentration camp and the dull, bleak, spiritual emptiness in the lives of Soviet citizens (like Wassilij's daughter). Rubashov, of course, justifies this - using Communist Dialectic (his theory of the "relative maturity of the masses"). His act is the dramatic "proof" of Koestler's contention: that Rubashov can see Gletkin and No. 1 as the spiritual sons of himself and Lenin, as the dialectical fulfillment of the relatively more human heroes of the Revolution (the men in the photograph) whom they are murdering now, proves that Communism is corrupt in its essential logic, not merely in certain casual historical manifestations.

Koestler does not work out in detail his thinking on the root error of the Communist movement. Nevertheless, it remains the most suggestive part of his book. During his interrogation by Gletkin, we are told that Rubashov would admit to anything which was "logically" consequent upon Rubashov's thought, even if Rubashov had not actually done it. This incident represents the suppression of reality by reason - with Communism representing the most extreme contemporary example. *Darkness at Noon* is the story of a man who tells a lie for the sake of an idea; the history of Communism, Koestler suggests dramatically in his novel, is the destruction and distortion of reality in order to confirm the mastery and the release from the constraints of the world which Communists experience in their ideology.

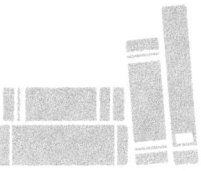

DARKNESS AT NOON

INTRODUCTION

As Koestler indicates in the note preceding the text, he composed the novel during the period October 1938-April 1940. He has described the circumstances under which the book was written in *Scum of the Earth* and in *The Invisible Writing*. The book was written in German - Koestler's only literary language at the time, since his native Hungarian had no commercial value outside of Hungary. The manuscript survived several searches of Koestler's apartment by the French police and a few months in a French concentration camp. Koestler worked on the translation with the translator, Daphne Hardy. In Koestler's escape from France in 1940 when the Nazi occupation began, the original manuscript was lost. The English translation therefore remains the closest thing existing to the original German. The current German edition is a translation of this English translation. The author himself read and corrected the page-proofs in an English prison while he waited for the status of his immigration to be established. He was still in prison when the book was published.

Darkness at Noon follows hard upon Koestler's open break with the Communist Party which he had served faithfully for seven years. He thus had done a good deal of "research" on the Communist mind. In addition, he had journeyed through the Soviet Union and seen the horrible conditions of life there. Further, he had met a few of the "stars" of the Moscow trials during that journey. He had been in prison in Spain and France. He had discovered from his friends Eva and Alexander Weissberg, who had been imprisoned in the U.S.S.R. by the Party, some of the techniques of interrogation and extracting confessions. The last and most famous of the Moscow Trials took place in 1938, but Koestler must have thought about the motives for the confessions for some time earlier. The first of the series of trials had been held in 1935.

Darkness at Noon sold only a few thousand copies when it first appeared in England. No doubt the main reason for this was that everyone's attention was turned to World War II. National Socialist Germany was the enemy and the Soviet Union was an ally. But when the war ended and Communism came to be seen for the enemy it was, Koestler's novel became an international best-seller and has remained one ever since. Controversy has always surrounded the book. Not only Communists and fellow-travelers were (and are) hostile to the novel, but many on the political left resented such uncompromising criticism of Communism and the Soviet Union. As late as 1962 John Strachey (the English Member of Parliament and former Labor Cabinet Minister) was characterizing the book as part of the "literature of reaction" and implying that its "anti-rationalism" was narrow-minded. In his autobiography Koestler tells of the destruction of an old friendship with a respected English public figure who could not accept the author's changing sides. What seems to be responsible for the animus with which the non-Communist Left received the book is the radical nature of Koestler's critique. It is not a particular implementer of policies, but the very nature of Communist (and, it seems to be implied, any) ideology that is rotten. This is too much for many "rationalists" to take. As George Orwell remarks in his perceptive essay on Koestler (*Collected Essays*, page 228), "The notion that So-and-so has 'betrayed,' that things have only gone wrong because of individual wickedness, is ever present in left-wing thought." When the French translation appeared in 1946, it set off violent attacks on the book and the author by the Communists and their sympathizers. Hundreds of thousands of copies of the book were sold - too many for the Party to buy and destroy, though it tried. In 1947 Merleau-Ponty, the French philosopher, wrote a book to defend the point of view of Gletkin and the entire course of Soviet history. Koestler's novel has been credited with being a decisive influence in the referendum on the French constitution of 1946. If the Communists had not been beaten in that referendum they would probably have controlled the government. Thus, *Darkness at Noon* has been (and continues to be) an event in a political struggle as well as a work of creative fiction.

Koestler's book takes its place in that tradition of political novels of which Dostoevsky's are the outstanding exemplars. In contemporary fiction it is also related to a number of anti-Utopian, anti-totalitarian fables of which Orwell's *1984* and Huxley's *Brave New World* are the best known. It is also one of many fictional studies of Communism which emerged especially after World War II. Manes Sperber's *The Burned Bramble* is one of the best of these representations of contemporary history and the contemporary political mind. In his identification of Communism's essential error as the idolization of "reason" Koestler participates in the critique of post-Renaissance rationalism which is the great **theme** running through Dostoevsky's books. Though not so profound as his great predecessor, in *Darkness at Noon*, Koestler is clearly of this school of thought.

The powerful impact the novel has had derives in the first instance from its lucid and subtle revelation of the Communist mind. But readers have sometimes missed the complex unity of **themes** in the novel; for the author combines an analysis of the logic behind the Moscow trials, and a general description of the Communist mind and the Communist Party, with a fictional history of the Party's activities in Europe in the Thirties, with a lucid expression of the fallacy of Communist rationalism. Koestler's dramatic statement of the proposition that the Communist ideology has sacrificed concrete living men for the sake of a creation of the mind, an idea, an abstraction - mankind - is thematically more important and intellectually more interesting than his hypothesis about why Bukharin and others confessed to the absurd charges of treason, espionage and anti-Communist activities.

The literary fate posterity may accord Arthur Koestler is uncertain now. Surely, future readers will not have the strange fascination of contemporary readers - who wish to read about the mentality that continues to determine historic events while they derive the aesthetic satisfaction offered by a tragic novel.

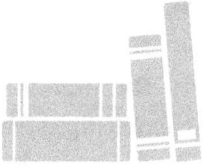

DARKNESS AT NOON

TEXTUAL ANALYSIS

PART I - THE FIRST HEARING

CHAPTERS I-V

It is 4 A.M., and Rubashov, a former Commissar of the People, is in his room dreaming of the first time he was arrested by the secret police of Germany in 1933. A picture of No. 1 hangs over his bed. The hand twitching in his sleep during this recurring nightmare indicates his dreaming of the difficulty he had in getting his arm through the sleeve of his bathrobe when the police burst in on him. Rubashov's deafness in one ear resulted from being hit over the head with a pistol at his arrest.

> Comment: The reader is meant to identify the men in Rubashov's dream with the German National Socialist (Nazi) Secret Police - the Gestapo. The National Socialists, and their leader, Hitler, were the sworn enemies of the German Communist Party (even though they had collaborated with it). When they came to power they ruthlessly exterminated

the Communist Party. Rubashov, though a foreigner (i.e., a Russian), was working with the German Party because all the Communist parties of the world were united under the Communist International with headquarters in Moscow. Even today, when Moscow no longer exercises absolute authority, the various Communist parties of the world compose an integral society; for whatever may divide them, they are united by history and ideology. Thus, any one Communist party's affairs are also the concern of the two giant parties, the Soviet and the Chinese.

The picture of "No. 1" obviously is of Josef Djugashwili (Stalin), the leader of the Communist Party of the Soviet Union.

Thus, it is immediately clear to the reader that the setting of the novel is a totalitarian country - a one-party state and a dictatorial regime. Although the terms "Communism" and "Soviet Union" are never mentioned in the book, there is no doubt that Koestler is writing an historical novel - about Communism, the Soviet Union, and Stalin. But though this is of great importance in understanding the author's intentions, the reader should realize that the conditions described in the novel could occur under any kind of totalitarian politics. The similarities between Rubashov's dream and his arrest in his own country are intended to point to the underlying similarity of the German National Socialist and Communist regimes, in spite of their mutual surface hostility.

This time, however, the hammering at his door keeps up even after he awakens. Two men from the Commissariat of the Interior have come to arrest Rubashov. Together with Vassilij, the porter, who had served in Rubashov's regiment during the civil war, and who idolizes Rubashov, they break into Rubashov's room. The older of the two men is respectful: he stands at attention in the presence of the hero of the Revolution. The younger man, however, is rude, harsh and itching to use his pistol.

Comment: The differences in attitudes of the two arresting officers towards Rubashov signal another theme of the story: the relatively humanistic vestiges in the make-up of the older, original revolutionists as opposed to the more brutal generation that has grown up under "socialism." It is significant that it is a man of this younger generation (Gletkin), which Rubashov and his comrades had "produced," who breaks Rubashov in the end.

Taken to his cell Rubashov notices the number 404 and his name on a card on the door: Nicolas Salmanovitch Rubashov. After inspecting the cell - it contains a bed, wash basin, a can that serves for a toilet - and looking out the window at the snow-covered yard, Rubashov puts his pince-nez (which he habitually rubs on his sleeve) and his cigarette butt carefully on the floor beside his bed. The prison warder looks through the peephole in the door at Rubashov, whose left hand is twitching in his sleep.

Comment: This small isolation cell is the main "set" of *Darkness at Noon*. Here, Koestler has achieved a perfect unity of theme, action and physical setting. Rubashov will leave his cell on several

occasions - actually, for interrogations and the like, and imaginatively, through day-dreams and reveries. But the main focus of attention is Rubashov's mind - his attempt to think things through. The isolation of the cell conforms perfectly to the privacy and intensity of Rubashov's speculations. And the physical prison is further symbolic of his intellectual confinement in the "cell" of his ideology.

The term "Commissar of the People" indicates that at one time he was high up in the political hierarchy of a Communist party in control of a country. He is therefore a prisoner for political reasons. The peephole in the door symbolizes the control that Rubashov's captors have over him, even though, in the isolation of his cell, he may attain the illusion of full freedom of mind.

CHAPTER VI

When the bugle awakens Rubashov in the morning, he realizes that he is in an isolation cell and will be shot. Rubashov is just one of the many of the "old guard," the Founding Fathers of the Revolution, who have been arrested by No. 1. Yet, even No. 1's victims and opponents in the Party cannot be sure that his policies are wrong.

> Comment: The arrest and execution of the heroes of the Revolution is not merely the theme of the "degeneration of the Revolution" after the revolutionists take power; for the totalitarianism of No. 1 and his Party - of Stalin, the Soviet Union and the Communist party - was brought into being, nurtured

and made possible by the revolutionary fathers themselves and their doctrine. Although Rubashov and others disapprove of No. 1, they cannot make a fundamental critique of his rule because they share the same ideology that No. 1 uses to rationalize his inhuman brutalities. They are therefore forced to adopt the judgment: Only "History" can judge - which really is a way of avoiding firm judgment.**

When Rubashov hears people coming down the corridor, he assumes it is for the routine beatings of the prisoners. But it is only breakfast. Through his peephole Rubashov can see cells 401 to 407 opposite. The sight of the bare, emaciated arms and hands of 407 reaching for his food disturbs Rubashov's memory.

Comment: The vague memory which the arms and hands of 407 evoke is the first significant sounding of a central theme in the story: Rubashov's humanity, the sense of human solidarity, some order of knowing and feeling quite beyond the reaches of Marxist-Leninist theory. This intimation of something beyond Party dogma is what makes Rubashov question the ruthless "rationalism" of Communism.

CHAPTER VII

When the breakfast detail omits him, Rubashov hammers on the door with his shoe. The warder and an officer (whose skull is shaved and has a large scar on it and who wears the ribbon of the Revolutionary Order in his buttonhole) then come in. The officer tells Rubashov that he was omitted because he had earlier reported that he had a toothache. When the door slams shut, Rubashov runs to the hole and cries for paper and a pencil.

> Comment: Although we are not told his name in this chapter, the officer with the shaved skull is a major character - in fact, Rubashov's adversary and interrogator, Gletkin. What begins here as an apparently casual encounter, is actually the first confrontation in a terrible struggle - between the old generation and the new, between Rubashov's individuality and Communist conformity, between autonomous intellect and feeling and Communist dogma.

CHAPTER VIII

Rubashov imagines that the officer sees him as a man who, though a hero of the Revolution, has now outlived his usefulness and has conspired against the Party leadership.

> Comment: Rubashov's conjecture about how the officer regards him anticipates the reasoning which Rubashov is ultimately persuaded to accept: whatever his past services to the Party, his current opposition to the leader has made him an "objective" danger to the state and he therefore deserves to be eliminated. This is the first mention of this important specimen of Communist "logic." Koestler continues to develop it with greater and greater elaborateness.

Then Rubashov's neighbor in 402 makes contact with him through the "quadratic alphabet" - a conventional prison code, whereby letters are tapped out according to position in a square grid. Rubashov is surprised to discover a genuine "counterrevolutionist" - i.e., a Czarist. 402 asks Rubashov to describe the woman he last slept with. But as he taps out his reply, Rubashov suddenly recalls what the cupped hands of 407 remind him off: a Pieta.

> Comment: 402's outlook and modes of thought are completely outside of Rubashov's ideology. The confrontation between the two indicates a simple human contact - transcending ideology; it also serves to make clear the radically untraditional nature of Rubashov's ideology (Communism). Koestler seems to have made 402 a Czarist "reactionary" in order to stress No. 1's culpability for the troubles of the country - the famine, the failure of other Communist revolutions. 402 is so obviously a "man from the past," that it seems ludicrous that men like him could be effective saboteurs of Communism.

A Pieta is a representation of the Blessed Virgin Mary mourning over the dead body of Jesus Christ (her son), who is usually held on her knees. It is a very popular theme of religious art. Pieta also means "pity" in Italian.

CHAPTER IX

Rubashov recalls the time when he met with the nineteen-year-old head of a Party group in the art museum of a German town. This was where he was so impressed with a drawing of a Pieta. The German National Socialists had just come to power and were smashing the Party. As the head of the Intelligence and Control Division of the Comintern, Rubashov came to dismiss young Richard from the Party for having substituted literature calling for collaboration with other forces of the German regime in the place of the unrealistic pamphlets the Central Committee in Moscow had sent him. In spite of himself, Rubashov hinted to Richard that he intended to denounce him to the Gestapo. Richard is crushed by the news of his expulsion from the Party. On the train after the interview, Rubashov had a bad toothache and dreamt that Richard was about to run him over with a train engine because he had "cheated" him. A week later Rubashov was arrested by the Gestapo.

> **Comment:** This is the first of three flashbacks which illuminate Rubashov's character, the source of his "deviationism" or "oppositionism," and the way the Party operates. Koestler makes the memory of the Pieta trigger the flashback and thereby invests the whole complex meaning of the episode in the image of the arms and cupped hands of the Virgin, because he wishes to show how another "logic" was working in Rubashov at the time, in addition to the Party "logic" which governed his sinister mission to Germany: that is, there is an element present in this episode which according to the "logic" of the Party should not be there - namely, Rubashov's unconscious guilt for what he and the Party are doing to Richard. The betrayal of the young Richard, for whom the Party had been church, family, political party, and army, stands for the Party's betrayal (and Rubashov's role in it) of so many ordinary members of the Party by imposing on them the iron discipline and cruel vengeance of the arbitrary and capricious Moscow will. The emphasis in this chapter, of course, is on Rubashov's unconscious guilt. It helps to explain how he was later motivated to oppose the policies of No. 1.

The human impulses which reveal themselves in Rubashov's guilty dream, the sense of human compassion which moves him to warn Richard that he will be denounced, the stirrings of human solidarity beneath all ideology - these remain submerged in Rubashov's mind and conduct despite the discipline and doctrine of the Party. His dim awareness of some measure transcending Party rules is thus symbolized by his interest in the Pieta. The Pieta stands for the sympathy and mercy which the Party cruelly denies to its members in the name of "Historical Necessity." The action of the novel largely consists in the conflict between the Party's doctrine that its end justifies any means and Rubashov's inchoate sense of the inviolable human substance. The tragedy is that Rubashov is drenched in the Marxist-Leninist dialectic; he lacks the intellectual tools with which to emerge from inhibiting, stultifying ideology.

Although the German National Socialist Workers Party (Nazis) are persecuting the Communists, Koestler demonstrates the similarity between the two apparently antagonistic parties. They are both totalitarian in their politics, brutal and ruthless in pursuit of their goals. That is why the author has Rubashov's daydreams interrupted by the noise of the beaten peasant in the corridor. The treatment of "enemies" of the Party is just as inhumane in the "socialist homeland" as in the Third Reich.

The account of the Party's behavior in this chapter is historically accurate. It refused to admit that it had experienced a devastating defeat in Germany. The German Communist Party was actually the most powerful in the world after that of the Soviet Union. It had vast publishing enterprises, great wealth and many members. Yet the National Socialists came to power and quickly reduced the Party to a hulk. In spite of this the Communist International refused to permit the German members to call for a radical reexamination of its doctrine and methods; it refused to collaborate with non-Communist socialist parties; it refused to let its members refer to the plain truths of the political situation; and it characteristically sacrificed any of its members who showed any individuality of thought. The Party Line is like a military order given in combat - to be obeyed unquestioningly, with death to the hesitant or disobedient. The Richard episode illustrates all this.

The author doubtless intends the reader to recall that the intransigent stance of the Communist Party soon changed to the flexible one of the "Popular Front," in which the Party offered to collaborate with other parties it had formerly vilified and fought. But to anticipate the Party Line (as Richard had done) even by several months could cost a member expulsion, or his life. And the Line is determined from the top, especially from Moscow; and it is designed to serve the interests of Moscow. It is because Rubashov is guilty of less than complete devotion to some of the methods of No. 1, that he is eventually shot. The Party requires "absolute faith." It is a changing tactical formation with an unchanging rule of discipline and devotion to the collective Party will.

Again, the Richard episode shows how crushed and helpless a person is who has completely cast his thinking and his life in the Party mould when he is without the Party. Rubashov's inability, later on, to mount an autonomous critique of the Party, i.e., from a point outside it - shows that he is as dependent and helpless as the pathetic Richard.

Arthur Koestler was himself a member of the German Communist Party (and therefore of the Communist International) for several years. In his autobiography (*The Invisible Writing*) he reports that the Communists often found it convenient to get rid of errant members by "denouncing" them to the Gestapo - i.e., to the so-called natural enemies of the Communist Party. Thus, the Richard episode sums up many traits of the Party.

CHAPTER X

Rubashov notices that a prisoner taking exercise keeps looking up at his window. He finds out from 402 that "Harelip" is a political prisoner, a Communist, and has cell 400. He was tortured by a steam bath the day before. Rubashov prides himself on his ability to resist torture; he has never confessed in prison. He confidently looks forward to his interrogation, and he tries to prepare himself for the "steam bath" by imagining what it is like. He puts out his cigarette on his hand.

> Comment: There is an irony in this chapter which reveals Rubashov's disadvantage. Although he has had a number of prison experiences, they have all been in non-Communist countries. His confidence is therefore short-sighted. For although Communist prisons employ torture just as the National Socialist ones do, they also have another kind of pressure at their command. Rubashov forgets that in the other

prisons he was in the hands of the enemy. Now he is in the hands of "comrades." His captives can therefore appeal to the "logic" and faith Rubashov shares with them. Thus, the irony of this chapter underscores the trap that Rubashov is in: it is not the prison and the threat of torture (he can handle that); rather it is the trap of ideology (this he does not yet see).

At the end of the chapter, Rubashov thinks of the dream of Richard and of how he will soon be paying for his past deeds.

Comment: One of the motifs running through the story is Rubashov's notion that he must pay and is paying for his past actions (good and bad). This is another piece of "un-Communist logic" - that which a Communist might regard as a mental aberration. It stands both for Rubashov's guilt and that "logic" that transcends dialectic.

CHAPTER XL

Rubashov has a craving for cigarettes, but he is not permitted to buy any. 402 tries in vain to send him some. Thinking of 402, Rubashov thinks that he would perform all the brutalities of the civil war (between the Communists and the Czarists) again today, even in the knowledge that No. 1 and his totalitarian terror would control the Party.

Comment: The thought that he would still do those things that have brought No. 1 to power shows the fatal "logic" from which Rubashov cannot escape and which traps him in the end. Whatever advances the

Revolution, the Communist cause, is just. Whatever retards it is unjust. Thus Rubashov cannot make an effective rational opposition to No. 1. The part of him which believes that the end does not justify any means is divorced from his consciousness, and cannot demolish the Leninist logic which permeates his mind.

In spite of his resistance to this impulse, Rubashov finds himself saying aloud that he will pay for his past actions. He is frightened for the first time.

Comment: It would appear that Rubashov is here "reading," what Koestler refers to in his autobiography as the "invisible writing"; that he is susceptible to what Koestler, following Freud, calls the "oceanic sense" (the phrase occurs frequently in Koestler's writings and appears in the next to the last chapter of *Darkness at Noon*). The point, of course, is that Marxist dialectics takes no account of such things except as aberrations. The notion that one must pay, suffer, for whatever one does, even when what one does is necessary, is certainly a religious or quasi-mystical one. The author wishes to emphasize the defect of rationalism like the Marxist dialectical-materialist ideology. The reader is meant to see that what the Communists would call "vestiges of bourgeois sentimentality" is in fact the saving grace of essential humanity which Rubashov has retained in spite of more than thirty years of Communist life. This interplay of "reason" or "logic" and the "oceanic sense" is a recurrent theme in the book.

CHAPTER XII

Haunted by the notion of "payment," Rubashov thinks of the famous photograph of the delegates to the First Party Congress. He is in it, and No. 1 [Stalin] and his predecessor [Lenin]. Most have been shot by No. 1.

> Comment: The passage in this chapter in which Rubashov meditates on the Party's tyranny and failure is highly lyrical - one of the most poignant moments in the book; for it sings eloquently of the "darkness at noon" - the slavery and brutality which followed the triumph of the "party of the people"; the terrible perversion of what had seemed to be noble ideals; the hatred the people have for what had at the time of the Soviet Revolution actually seemed to many all over the world - including many non-Communists - the hope of the alienated masses. This is the paradox with which the book deals. It is the paradox in Rubashov's own life and he is fully conscious of it - though he never becomes fully aware of its source (this is why he is a pathetic figure). The paradox is the reason for Rubashov's guilt; and his guilt has to be that of the Party as well, since he had no life away from the Party.
>
> Thus, we see that throughout the first part of the novel and most of the second half Rubashov is trying to explain this apparent incongruence: the Party which embodies the "Will of History" has produced virtually nothing but misery and failure. The proof of this is the fact that so many fathers of the Revolution have been shot by No. 1, the second great leader of the Party. Rubashov himself, one of the very great heroes

of the Revolution, who served the cause faithfully all his life, winds up now in a prison awaiting a bullet in the back of his head. The frequent reference in the book to the light patch on the walls of rooms where the famous photograph had hung is a continual reminder of the "darkness at noon" - the failure of the Party. It is difficult for a young American living today to understand this situation. It is as if American citizens were suddenly told - in 1805 or 1815 - that the Founding Fathers of the Republic had become traitors; as if their names and pictures were suddenly no longer in evidence; as if those still alive were shot after publicly confessing their crimes at "show trials." The Great Purge which Stalin carried on in the thirties was a traumatic experience for Communists and their sympathizers all over the world. It is no wonder that Rubashov is so confused. And now it is his turn to be denounced as a traitor. Only by experiencing imaginatively the shock of the Great Purge can the reader understand Rubashov's compulsion to figure out what went wrong.

After he got out of the German prison, Rubashov took a mission to Belgium to see that the Communist dockworkers complied with the Party's new order to unload oil for Fascist Italy. (A few years before, the Party had made a similar reversal when Germany was involved.) The devoted, naive, Communist workers, led by Little Loewy, rebelliously upbraided Rubashov. But the Russian ships steamed into the harbor and Rubashov had Loewy denounced by the Party as an enemy agent - even though he felt guilty for what he did and for Loewy's past suffering because of Party ineptitude. He later dreamed that he was breaking Loewy's back over his knee. Loewy committed suicide a few days later.

Comment: The purpose of the second of the three flashbacks that are enacted in Rubashov's daydreams is to represent the doubts about the Party's course which have beset Rubashov in recent years and which (together with No. 1's paranoia) have resulted in his arrest. More important, this ultimate crisis in his life stirs up these memories of scenes that stand for his own guilt and the Party's, his betrayal of the people for whom the Party had been everything. These scenes stand for the Party's failure. And these memories accompany Rubashov's reawakened and sharpened "oceanic sense" - the spring of charity and human solidarity - because they were occasions when, vaguely and reluctantly, he sensed that there was something wrong with his Party mission. Thus, the Little Loewy interlude is symbolic of the general corruption, cynicism, opportunism and ingratitude of the Party. That is why Rubashov feels uneasy when Loewy tells him his life story, why Rubashov has a nightmare just as he did after the Richard affair.

But the complicated, highly intellectual Rubashov's devotion to the twists and turns of the Party Line is in sharp contrast to the courageous and clear-sighted refusal of Loewy and the simple dockworkers to accept the Party's new order. Again, the situation is analogous to the Richard episode: Richard too was idealistic, and his idealism led him to desert the Party Line - though neither he nor Loewy deserted the Party. Rather, the Party deserted them. In these two vignettes Koestler gives an imaginative representation, in the moral terms of individual human beings, of historical events.

The Soviet Union did, in fact, trade with its so-called neutral enemy Fascist Italy (as it traded with National Socialist Germany). It thus directly aided the Italian conquest of Ethiopia. The reader is no doubt meant to recall that a few years after the **episode** described in this chapter, the Soviet Union and National Socialist Germany concluded a secret treaty which called for the partition of Poland and the Baltic states. Communist hypocrisy, the unwillingness of the Soviet Union to make the material sacrifices an embargo of Italy and Germany would have entailed, the betrayal of the idealism and devotion of its best partisans abroad - all this is dramatically embodied in the Little Loewy episode.

Of much greater significance than the cynical opportunism of the Party is the way in which the whole affair is handled. It tells us the nature of the Party. The sudden reversal of the "Line" is decided without reference to the feelings, ideas or position of the local Party members. Rational dissent is not permitted. Enthusiastic submission to the will of the Party is expected. The only alternative is dismissal from the Party - and, frequently, as we see in this chapter, public vilification, or, sometimes, assassination or execution. The Party recognizes no debt for past deeds. No allowance is made for a "legal opposition." As in the case of the men in the photograph, Loewy and his comrades are sacrificed without compunction. As always, the end - whatever the Party decides it to be - justifies the means.

The cumulative effect of events like the Little Loewy **episode** has been to produce the burden of guilt and doubt which have gotten Rubashov where he is now.

Of course, to an orthodox Communist, such action as described in this chapter does not constitute a "betrayal" of

Party members or any hypocrisy. Anything which promotes the welfare of the Home of the Revolution is justified and moral. The individual is just fodder for the mill of the movement. Some people actually argued this way when *Darkness at Noon* was published! But the reader is meant to see that the Party says one thing and does another, that it talks of noble acts, but will compromise its high-sounding declarations for profit.

CHAPTERS XIII-XIV

Rubashov is taken to the doctor for his toothache but won't undergo an operation without anesthetics. He thinks of Richard and Little Loewy, of how the Communist movement in its winding course destroys its members.

> **Comment: In this chapter as elsewhere, Koestler has Rubashov put his finger on that aspect of the Communist movement which has been nagging at his sense of human dignity for many years: the individual does not matter. The individual is nothing; the movement, everything. For Rubashov the real terror of his imprisonment by the Party is that he now is driven to come face-to-face, self-consciously, with his hitherto half-concealed doubts.**

Rubashov begins his payment on the fifth day. His first interrogation is conducted by his civil war comrade, Ivanov, who begs Rubashov to confess to part of the charges against him and cooperate in a show trial, so that he can perhaps get him off with a prison term with eventual amnesty. (No recording secretary is present.) Rubashov refuses, but Ivanov gives him a fortnight to think it over. Ivanov's conversation reveals that in the past few years Rubashov reluctantly denounced people on trial for opposition (including Arlova, his former secretary, and some of the men from the photograph) and affirmed his loyalty to No. 1. Ivanov charges that Rubashov did it in order to be able to work for his own policy in opposition to No. 1. Now, Rubashov is charged (falsely) with plotting the assassination of No. 1. When Rubashov says that the Party has destroyed the promise of the Revolution, Ivanov points out that Rubashov refers to the Party as "you" - as something apart from himself

> **Comment: The first part of the novel has been occupied with unfolding those events in Rubashov's past which motivate his sense of personal guilt and his doubts about the Party. The incidents add to the dramatic excitement because each one is a more shocking example of human baseness. Richard was an honest, idealistic Party worker; Loewy was a sophisticated, shrewd, efficient and experienced local leader who had accomplished a great deal with his dockworkers section; Arlova was Rubashov's mistress. Each incident involves betrayal of innocent members of the Party; but the depth of personal and Party treachery is greater in each succeeding case. The fact that Rubashov himself - obviously one of the more humane and idealistic of the Party leaders - played a role in the "liquidation" of some of the Fathers of the Revolution demonstrates perhaps more clearly than anything else the decadence of the Party; for Rubashov's corruption is the Party's corruption. The implication is that the most that the "opposition" did was to express their disapproval of some of No. 1's policies. Again, the novel is faithful to the historical record: It is beyond doubt that the great Party leaders Stalin had tried and executed were not guilty of treason to his policies. Rather,**

Stalin was consolidating his absolute power over Party and State. It is important for the reader to see that Rubashov's attitude to the Party and No. 1 is confused. When he bitterly criticizes the Party, the reader should recall that Rubashov previously said that he would still work to bring No. 1 to power if he had to do it all again. Rubashov's primary attitude seems to be disappointment at the Party for not being true to itself. To its original motivating insights and ideals as embodied in the delegates to the First Party Congress. The Party did not usher in an era of human joy, but of human suffering; and the chief sufferers have been the Party's own: the masses and the Party faithful. However, at this point, Rubashov does not appear to have followed the impulses which we have seen working in the flashbacks-impulses, feelings of charity and guilt, which are not part of the closed system of thought and action which the Party embodies - to their logical conclusion: in other words, he has not, as Part I of the novel concludes, made, under the influence of his feelings, a radical critique of the very premises of Party doctrine' - even though this radical critique is implied in the doubts which have grown in his mind over the past few years. Hence, his confusion. He is still a Communist; but being a Communist disturbs him profoundly. The questions which the reader should ask, therefore, are: How far will Rubashov go in his break with the Party? Will he break with basic Party doctrine as well? That is, will he conclude that he and the Party have been wrong from the beginning, and that No. 1 is not just an unfortunate accident? Will he break with dialectical materialism, the philosophy of Communism? Or, after forty years, is his intellect so permeated with the Communist mode of thought and his will so habituated to the Communist drive for power that he cannot break the mould in spite of intimations of "something more deeply interfused"? To ask these questions is to state some of the chief themes of the novel, as well as to summarize the nature of Rubashov's entrapment.

The dogmatic suppression of the "I" - the ego, the individual, autonomous person - is an important theme introduced in this chapter when Ivanov observes that Rubashov is no longer speaking of the Party as - "we" but as "you" - thereby distinguishing himself from it. This theme comes to dominate much of the book.

Ivanov's review of Rubashov's career in this chapter covers the history of Stalin's Great Purge, the chronology of which Koestler follows closely. Stalin's purge, like No. 1's, went on throughout the 1930's. It affected the membership of all Communist parties, including the Communist Party of the United States.

Why does Rubashov not take up Ivanov's appeal to "reason" and sign a "partial confession" in order to have his life? The answer to this question explains much about Rubashov's character and the structure of the novel; two different explanations may be given: 1) Rubashov's growing doubts over the last few years represent a flight from the Party's "logic" and "reason" to a different order of experience; 2) for Rubashov to play Ivanov's game now would be to leave unresolved Rubashov's problems with the course of post-Party history - even though it might save his life; a man with Rubashov's passion for intellectual comprehension needs to see how this period, including his imprisonment and the state of the Party, fits into the logic of history; what he seeks now is not to escape death, but to reconcile his own vision of the Revolution with what has happened to it and the Party in the last twenty years. The first movement of the novel has led up to this intellectual exercise by revealing the concrete problem, the particular sources of Rubashov's doubt and confusion.

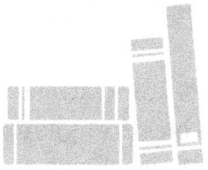

DARKNESS AT NOON

TEXTUAL ANALYSIS

PART II - THE SECOND HEARING

CHAPTER I

After his interrogation Rubashov writes in his diary a meditation on the principles - the "logic" - of the Party and his place in it. In order to apply the ruthless "logic" of Party theory-and-action, you must have faith that the judgment of "History" will confirm your own. And Rubashov, unlike No. 1, lacks this confidence which is the only thing which can sustain a man who disagrees with his fellow Communists.

> **Comment: This chapter compresses many insights about Communism in a few pages and simultaneously exposes the dilemma of the party leader who would oppose the controlling Party clique. Rubashov is not even sure that No. 1 is wrong! This is the measure of his confusion and of the depth of his Communist faith. The problem is not confined to just an isolated individual; it is inherent in Communism itself: any**

Communist who would criticize an action of the Communist Party on the grounds of traditional moral ethics must first ask if the act is conducive to the welfare of the Party. If he cannot answer the question, he will be plunged into confusion and despair - where Rubashov is now.

Koestler's understanding of Communism grows more explicit as the book progresses. It adds up to the indictment made by other ex-Communists like Frank Meyer and Whittaker Chambers and scholars like Eric Voegelin: Communism is the glorification of human reason which, having plunked the meaning of history, has the right and duty to work out its hypotheses no matter how terrible their side effects.

CHAPTER II

Ivanov and Gletkin (the officer with the scar on his shaven skull) argue about the proper treatment for Rubashov. Gletkin is for physical pressure, which will work on any man. But Ivanov - his superior - says that all Rubashov requires is cigarettes, pencil, paper, time and appeal to "logic"; then he will give in. Gletkin has illusions about the eventual transformation of human nature under the influence of Socialism. Ivanov does not.

> Comment: The argument between Ivanov and Gletkin is actually another embodiment of a theme encountered elsewhere in the book: the conflict of the generations (quite apart from the clash of personalities). Ivanov thinks. He is a apart from the clash of personalities) Ivanov thinks. He is a man very much like Rubashov. Gletkin, on the other hand,

does not think - not in the same sense. He is a product of the Revolution, which nursed and educated him for the task of the immediate consolidation of the Revolution - a task which requires brutality and blind faith. Ivanov's "logic" and cynicism mark him as a man of the pre-Revolution generation which had to think things through for itself because it was living in a "hostile, capitalist world." That is why Ivanov has a good deal of sympathy for Rubashov and Gletkin has not.

CHAPTER III

Rubashov resolves to spend the remaining fortnight in a written attempt to make sense of things. He is fascinated to discover his autonomous ego, which seems to have lived a life apart from his conscious, Communist "reason," speaks the language of emotional memories (the flashbacks) and believes in payment for past deeds. He daydreams of Arlova, his former secretary and mistress, when he was the head of a Trade Delegation abroad. She had been unjustly tried for treason.

> Comment: Arlova's story (the third important flashback) takes its place alongside of Richard's and Little Loewy's: a poignant example of how the Party betrays and destroys individuals.
>
> In order to show what Communism does to the individual soul, Koestler employs a brilliant device which at once realistically conveys the desperation of the prisoner and the intense relationship of the member to the Party. He prepared for the introduction of it here by having Ivanov point out

in the "first hearing" that Rubashov was calling the Party "you." What he calls in this chapter "the grammatical fiction" is not merely a random deviation from the collective Party will, but rather, apparently, an irreducible part of a person's identity - outside the categories of Communist dialectic and beyond its control, surviving the corruptions of its ideology. Actually, all the nonrational or emotional experiences Rubashov has had in the book have been manifestations of this "grammatical fiction." It is one of the controlling symbols of the book.

Rubashov's toothache, which has been with him intermittently for many years and was always aggravated in moments of stress, seems to be a kind of physical analogue of the pain of memory in him.

CHAPTERS IV-V

402 informs Rubashov that his new neighbor, 406, had been a member of a post-World War I East European revolutionary commune and therefore was put in prison for twenty years. When released he immediately took a train to the Home of the Party and was thrust into the cell next to Rubashov's a few days after arriving. Now mentally deranged, he can only keep tapping out "Arise, ye nations of the earth." When taking exercise with Rubashov he draws a map of the country (U.S.S.R.), claims that he must have gotten on the wrong train, and suggests that the same thing may have happened to Rubashov.

Comment: 406 performs the same function as - Little Loewy, the dockworkers, Arlova and Richard. He too stands for all those who have been cheated by the Party. The reason Koestler introduces him after all the others is that 406 has nothing to do with Rubashov's own history; he is not a person out of his past. Therefore, his is a piece of independent testimony to the case against the Party. The line that he obsessively mutters and taps out - "Arise, ye wretched of the earth" - is the first line of the International, the Communist hymn. It was originally written in French in 1871, but there are versions in virtually every language. The first verse and refrain of the English version follow:

Arise, ye prisoners of starvation,
Arise, ye wretched of the earth,
For justice thunders condemnation,
A better world's in birth.

Tis the final conflict,
Let each stand in his place,
The International [i.e., the International Party]
Shall be the human race.

This song and the first country of the Communist Revolution, the U.S.S.R., the outline of which 406 draws obsessively, symbolize the Utopian and apocalyptic hope so many - including Rubashov, 406 and the others - had in the Party and the Soviet Union. But not only did the U.S.S.R. fail even to approach the realization of these hopes, the Party has shown no regard for the pathetic trust of people like 406.

406's position is poignantly and ironically analogous to Rubashov's. Both are intellectuals. Both are shocked by the tyranny and total failure of the Party, and the Party's Home. In each case the experience is traumatic. But 406 goes out of his mind, while Rubashov tries to "figure it out." Nevertheless, there is as much desperation in Rubashov's reaction as in the insane 406's. There is a depth of irony in the old prisoner's telling Rubashov that he was put on the wrong train and in his suggesting that the same thing happened to Rubashov: the deranged man's remark underlines Rubashov's plight; for the Party has failed to take its members to the promised destination; perhaps it was a "wrong train" going to a dreadful country. Of course, Koestler means for the reader also to ask if the right country - the Utopian vision of Communism - exists at all. The answer to this question is suggested in Part IV.

Koestler is undoubtedly alluding in this chapter to the Hungarian Commune - or Communist Revolution which ruled Hungary from March to July 1919 under Bela Kun who later died in the Purge in the Soviet Union. Koestler was a high school student at the time and the experience may have affected his future political drift towards Zionism and Communism.

When Rubashov is taken to be shaved, the barber passes along to him a note urging him to die without "confessing." Rubashov decides that this notion of honor is absurd for a Communist who has denounced the innocent and the loved in order to be able still to go on fighting for the correct Party Line.

Comment: The episode of the note urging Rubashov to die in silence raises the question of "honor" - one of the chief versions of the theme of the book. It helps to make clear how radically different Communist ethics are from traditional Western ethics. The individual has an inherent worth and dignity, and the end does not justify the means. But for the Communist the only thing that matters is to be on the side of "History" - to do the work of "History." This is why the note, which would appeal to the Czarist 402, does not touch Rubashov.

CHAPTERS VI-VII

From 402 Rubashov finds out that 380, Bogrov, former Commander of the Eastern fleet, is to be executed. All the prisoners line up in their cells drumming on their doors watching for the prisoner to pass. Bogrov had been in exile with Rubashov and was extremely devoted to him. Rubashov sees him dragged by and hears him call out his name loudly; Rubashov is physically and emotionally shaken. Ivanov then comes to his cell and tells him that Bogrov had taken the wrong stand on submarine construction, was tortured and refused to "confess" for a show trial.

> **Comment: There were hundreds of cases like Bogrov's in the thirties in Russia, not to mention the thousands of less important people who were shot or imprisoned. Aside from the meaning his torture and execution have for Rubashov, the point of Bogrov's death is that where in other countries people merely lose their jobs, for the same act they are executed in the Soviet Union. The reason for this is not merely that it is a dictatorship, but that in a Communist country the stakes of any action - be it in art, or engineering, or science, or politics - are always on the highest level; for every action is "political,"**

every event may be of great historical importance, charged with apocalyptic significance. One is not merely bungling a job; one may be fighting the inexorable dialectic of "History." Death is therefore a reasonable penalty. Every year hundreds of persons are executed in the Soviet Union for "economic crimes" - actions that would be perfectly legal in the West, or perhaps warrant a few years in prison or a fine. Art is censored as nowhere else; writers go to prison for deviations from the Line; the Party understands that in order to succeed it must have captive minds as well as captive bodies. Like 406, Bogrov's appearance offers the reader independent evidence of the terror of Communism.

When Rubashov accuses Ivanov of having stage-managed the whole episode with Bogrov in order to shake him into signing a confession, Ivanov says that it was Gletkin's doing. They then argue about the total tyranny and regression of the country. Ivanov proudly sanctions everything by maintaining that the future of Communism justifies anything. He rebukes Rubashov for giving in to the temptations of pity and guilt. Rubashov sums up his dilemma by asking himself if he would be willing to send Arlova to her death again. Ivanov leaves Rubashov and goes to Gletkin, who rebukes him for his stupidity in setting up a scene which could only cause Rubashov to refuse to confess. But Ivanov predicts that now that he has rectified the error by appealing to Rubashov's Communist "logic"; he will sign in the morning.

Comment: The scene in which Rubashov hears Bogrov call out his name has all the shock of stage melodrama. But since it has been stage-managed by Gletkin, Koestler is able both to reap the novelistic benefits of melodrama and avoid the dangers of its crudeness. The argument between Ivanov and Rubashov about the history of the Party, about ends and means, summarizes comprehensively the dilemma Rubashov finds himself in. It is just as much charged with drama as the previous scene with Bogrov. Communist doctrine as Ivanov speaks it is rendered by Koestler with superb fidelity and sophistication. The striking thing about the argument between the two friends is that Rubashov cannot argue with Ivanov. The implicit assumption is that reason is all on Ivanov's side. Rubashov can only protest with irrational sentiment. In fact, Ivanov's voice is virtually Rubashov's own. It should be clear to the reader that Ivanov's "reason" is based on faith, on the Communist vision of the future and the "laws" of history, that it is fundamentally irrational. But Rubashov cannot see this; he is caught between Communist "reason" and his human feelings. Although Rubashov has not progressed beyond the emotional and intellectual stalemate of the earlier chapters, the discussion with Ivanov, coming as it does after so much emotional tension, forces Rubashov to make a decision on the problem he has been defining and redefining throughout the book. This is the turning point in the action.

The long catalogue of almost incredible social and political and economic evils that Rubashov recites to Ivanov in criticism of the Home of the Revolution is an accurate description of the state of the Soviet Union in the 1930's, and in its essence is applicable today as well.

DARKNESS AT NOON

TEXTUAL ANALYSIS

PART III - THE THIRD HEARING

CHAPTERS I-III

Rubashov tells 402 that he decided to give in. 402 finds this dishonorable, but to Rubashov it is highly honorable. On the morning after Ivanov's visit Rubashov wrote out in his diary what he had "figured out." Opposition to tyranny is foolish because "History" requires tyranny. With every new development of technology or social and economic organization, the masses are left in a state of political immaturity requiring a ruthless political tutelage before an increase in freedom can come. That is what No. 1 - who is only a manifestation of "History's laws" - is doing. The sensible thing for members of the opposition like Rubashov to do, therefore, is cooperate with No. 1 in making the Revolution fully secure. Rubashov sends off a statement of his theory along with an agreement to cooperate in a show trial. He looks forward to being able to develop his theory at leisure in a great book after the trial.

Comment: The first half of the book amply demonstrated that Rubashov is unable - philosophically, rationally, logically - to overcome the ideological dialectic. His feelings have not been able to dissolve forty years of Communist thinking - even though the terrible tyranny of the U.S.S.R. has shaken that thinking to the point of confusion and despair. It is thus inevitable that Ivanov's "logic" appears irresistible to Rubashov; this is his pathos and his tragedy. This is what Koestler suggests motivated the incredible public confessions to sabotage and treason of so many sophisticated revolutionists in the various purges of the Communist countries. One could sum up the whole tragedy by saying: they (like Rubashov) were Communists to the end!

In his autobiography Koestler states that he, like other Communist intellectuals, had a kind of private Marxism-Leninism to help buttress the public version. In this way apparent anomalies and unpleasant practices by the Party and the U.S.S.R. could be explained away. It would appear that Rubashov's "law of relative maturity" is a case of this private rationalization - well-integrated, of course, with Marxist-Leninism. It satisfies the psychological need for a full and complete understanding of events without having to give up the first principles of Communism. This is Rubashov's way of preserving his sanity (think of 406) and his faith. Communist tyranny and the promise of Communist freedom are thus fully reconciled in his mind in an "Historical" theory.

Rubashov's disagreement with 402 on the subject of honor and his theory of the process of maturation of the "masses" illuminate nicely the materialism of Communism. (Materialism is that philosophy which holds that matter is the only reality; everything, including thought, will and feeling can be explained only in the terms of matter.) For Rubashov honor is tied to "use" - to concrete political effectiveness, to pragmatic action. For 402 honor has nothing to do with "use"; it is based on conforming to an image of man completely unrelated to economic or political action. Thus 402 would rather die than debase himself confessing to crimes he did not commit. And Rubashov's explanation of social phenomena - the "maturity" of the people ("masses") - is utterly dependent on technology and industry. The Communist image of man, Communist ideals, are completely materialistic.

In order fully to understand these chapters, the reader should ask the question: Does Rubashov give in because he sees that he was wrong in his opposition to No. 1's policies; or does he, the opposition having failed, see nothing to be gained by any further opposition? First of all, he does retain his intellectual autonomy by offering his own explanation of history, and by not pleading guilty to the specific false charges against him, and by treating No. 1 as an historical "phenomenon." Secondly, he does admit that No. 1 is right about the necessity for an iron rule at this time in order to conserve the Revolution; freedom is impossible. (In fact, No. 1 has been evolved by History for this purpose!) This does not mean that there is no room for disagreement over particular policies and measures, but it means that it is wrong to fight against the basic policy of repression. (Rubashov has done this - though not through treason, sabotage, attempted assassination or plotting; he merely had his opinion!) Rubashov now sees, therefore, that, however right he might have been in questions of detail, he was fundamentally wrong in wanting a more democratic and humanitarian regime. And when caught, however unfairly, as an "oppositionist," it would be foolish not to help advance the basic policy of the regime and remain in the Party by cooperating in propaganda of No. 1's necessary work. Even today, many leftists view Stalin's reign of terror as a necessary one. For example Lelio Basso, the famous Italian Marxist, speaks of the horrors of that day as "shadows cast by the light of the Revolution."

In the exercise yard Rubashov meets a peasant who has been sentenced to ten years imprisonment as a reactionary because he resisted the regime's modernization measures. Rubashov regards him coldly, in the light of his new theory.

> Comment: The introduction of the simple-minded peasant helps to make more comprehensive the view of Communist stupidity and ruthlessness that Koestler has been presenting. It also dramatically emphasizes the change in Rubashov. Before the visit from Ivanov he would probably have taken the peasant's fate as another indictment of the regime. Now the peasant is merely a confirmation of Rubashov's "law of the lag" in the development of the masses after a significant change in industry or social organization. This scene helps the reader to see how the Communists justify what appears to the non-Communist as political terror.

CHAPTERS III-VI

Ivanov is arrested and shot, and Gletkin takes his place as Rubashov's interrogator. Although Rubashov had declared his readiness to publicly renounce his "objectively" counterrevolutionary attitudes of opposition to No. 1's direction, he is not prepared to confess to the fantastic charges of which he is accused. But after a series of interrogation sessions over a span of days during which he is allowed very little sleep, kept in the glare of a lamp, and relentlessly pursued by Gletkin's logic, Rubashov comes to sign a series of confessions to these various charges - which include treason, sabotage, a plot to poison No. 1 and counterrevolutionary goals. He does this even in the knowledge that the Party intends to execute him after the show trial. Gletkin wins his arguments by first "proving" that Rubashov had for years been one of those in opposition to the Party Line. Rubashov is confronted with the tortured "Harelip," who turns out to be Michael Kieffer, the son of one of Rubashov's old friends, himself an executed hero of the Revolution. Harelip reports that Rubashov had talked to his father about the necessity of working against the policies of No. 1 [true] and had engaged him to poison No. 1 [false]. Gletkin reminds Rubashov of an (idle) conversation he had had with a certain Herr von Z. about the possibility of a revolution against No. 1. Apparently, Herr von Z. had been in the employ of No. 1, setting a trap for Rubashov. Gletkin is able to get Rubashov to agree to building a dialectical bridge between these facts about Rubashov's attitudes and the specific false accusations. For whether or not Rubashov actually performed the deeds of which he is accused, his attitudes imply sanction of such acts. The reason for this gross exaggeration of Rubashov's opposition is the need to justify the regime of No. 1, to discourage all opposition, and to offer to the people something so simple that they can readily understand it. Since Rubashov has now justified No. 1's regime to himself, his own logic forces him to assent to the argument which Gletkin calls his assignment from the Party, in order to make amends for the harm the opposition (which did not appreciate the necessity for No. 1's policies) has done to Party unity. Rubashov considers that one day when the Revolution is in no danger, the real truth may be told about him and the service he is performing. Rubashov now sees that the Gletkins - the cold-blooded, crude children of the Revolution - are just what the country needs. (Rubanshov's "pre-Revolutionary" humanitarian impulses are dangerous.)

> **Comment: There is a certain irony in the congratulations Gletkin receives from the recording secretary at the end of the interrogation. Gletkin thinks that he pressured Rubashov into confessing, but actually the credit belongs to Ivanov. It was Ivanov's tactics (see** Part II, **especially, the last chapter) which set Rubashov up for the "third hearing. "Once Rubashov gives in to "logic," (Part III, Chapter I) the rest follows; for it is implicit in his justification of No. 1, in his self-admission that he (Rubashov) has been wrong, that he will confess to any lie about himself if it will help the Party. (And these lies are the consequence in action of Rubashov's attitude.) The span between the general statement and confession he agrees to (in Part III, Chapter I) and the specific confessions Gletkin leads him to make is thus "dialectically," "logically," very slight.**
>
> **This point is worth dwelling on, for it illuminates the totalitarian aspect of Communist "logic." Subjective state of mind, the actual intention of the agent, so important in traditional Western ethics, is irrelevant in the Communist view. If you think it; if you say**

it; if you write it; if you do it - all these variations are so closely bound up for a Communist that the all-important distinctions among them are very easily lost. Communism's vision of a Utopian society is something to be achieved through immediate political action; and not just through patient use of traditional political means, but with a ruthless social engineering. This is the significance of the expression that appears so often in the novel: "We were consequent" - that is, We thought it, We said it, We wrote it, and We did it - regardless of the cost. Thus, it is easy for Communists to regard counterrevolutionary thought as if it were counterrevolutionary action. "Dialectically" thought is action. And so Rubashov, whose every premise is Communistic, must concede that if he did not actually resort to violence in order to oppose No. 1, he "ought" to have and didn't because of weakness. (It is a crowning irony that Rubashov "confesses" to having had anti-Communist - i.e., anti-revolutionary motives - and he does this for Communist motives.)

Readers frequently conclude that Rubashov has played the game and lost, and, as a good Communist, decides to make a gesture on behalf of Party unity at the end. But observe that this is the third time that Rubashov will have testified at a trial of the opposition. And whereas before, he denounced others - including the completely innocent Arlova - in order to be able to stay free to work in the Party on behalf of his own ideas, this time he is confessing because he has given up opposition; he has become convinced that opposition was wrong, that he was "sentimental." Thus, the question he asked himself during Ivanov's visit to his cell (Would he sacrifice Arlova again) can be answered by the reader now. Yes, he would sacrifice Arlova again; but for a different reason, for No. 1's reason - as a prop in an elaborate scenario for the benefit of the masses, as a way of discouraging opposition. (At least, it is suggested that this would be Rubashov's probable response; for although Arlova was not even "objectively" guilty of opposition, if the Party and No. 1 found it useful to eliminate her, Rubashov would certainly approve of the end in view.)

Koestler leaves the reason for Ivanov's execution vague. But the reader will probably not be far from the truth if he guesses that Gletkin's rivalry with and fear of Ivanov (a man very like Rubashov in his habits of mind) prompted him to report Ivanov for not really being serious about trapping Rubashov.

Writing in 1938-40, Koestler has Gletkin say that one day, after the Revolution has been made completely secure, the real service that people like Rubashov did for the Party in confessing to deeds they did not perform will be made known and they will be at least partially restored to public sympathy. In 1956, in his famous attack on Stalin, Khrushchev did just that! Recent years have seen the "rehabilitation" of many of the victims of Stalin's Purge.

When Gletkin identifies Rubashov and the opposition as not seeing the necessity for concentrating the Party's effort on consolidating the Revolution and as wanting instead to promote Revolution elsewhere, Koestler is alluding to the Trotsky-Stalin ideological split. Trotsky, the builder of the Red Army and one of the Great Communist dialecticians, broke with Stalin on this question, maintaining that the Party ought to concentrate on spreading the Communist Revolution around the world immediately. Stalin said that this goal should be postponed until the Revolution was fully consolidated in the U.S.S.R. His line was translated into a slogan which had a convenient double meaning (one for Communists and one for non-Communists): he said that the Soviet Union was merely building "Socialism in one Country," i.e., coexisting peacefully.

It is important to note that though Rubashov has worked things out in his theory of "relative maturity of the masses," his old thinking and sentiment still causes conflict. Koestler wishes to be faithful to the picture he drew of powerful "non-Communist" feelings and impulses. These - the I, "the grammatical fiction" - just cannot be expected to be dissipated all at once. Therefore, Rubashov's confusion persists and crops out intermittently, even after he concludes that opposition to No. 1's methods was wrong. Further, this will permit Koestler to suggest a more profound critique of Communism in Part IV.

It has been noted previously that Rubashov was tortured by the paradox of "darkness at noon." His attitude at the end of Part III now is that No. 1's "darkness" is necessary.

Gletkin's command of dialectic in Part III may appear to be contrary to his initial description as non-intellectual and crude. Nevertheless, he does retain his outstanding trait - cold-blooded devotion to No. 1 and his methods. And his view of things lacks the complexity and creativity of Rubashov's and Ivanov's - though it is essentially the same as theirs. It may be relevant here to mention that Koestler states in his autobiography that Marxist-Leninist jargon enables idiots to sound like intellectuals. Communism is really the simplest of philosophies embodied in the most complex of mass movements and forms of political warfare.

DARKNESS AT NOON

TEXTUAL ANALYSIS

PART IV - THE GRAMMATICAL FICTION

CHAPTER I

Wassilij's daughter reads the newspaper account to him. Rubashov had fully conformed to the plan that he and Gletkin had laid out, pleading guilty to all charges, holding himself up as a warning to anyone in the country who might in the least want to oppose the Party leadership. His only wish is to die after having at least acknowledged his repentance and confessed his sins against the Party and the masses. Though Wassilij signs his daughter's petition requesting death for those on trial, he observes that nowadays decency and cleverness are not found together.

> **Comment: By having the trial reported to the reader indirectly, Koestler is able to demonstrate how the trial of the great hero of the Revolution affects two very ordinary citizens. Wassilij and his daughter represent significant segments of the population.**

His daughter is typical of the militant nonintellectual devotees of Communism. She swallows the proceedings whole, just as the Party expects the "masses" to.

Because of millions like her, Stalin's numerous and grotesque show trials are a complete success, generating hatred of the "opposition." Making the defendants confess to heinous crimes they did not commit enables the "masses" to see the evil in the opposition. But Koestler makes her "reactionary" father (whose mentality is not very far from that of the peasant Rubashov encountered in prison) react in a much more thoughtful way. He penetrates to the heart of the problem of Communism: simple "decency" is outlawed for the sake of "cleverness." And no doubt there are millions like Wassilij in the country who will pay for their "reactionary" attitudes. The contrast between the gullible daughter crying for blood, a puppet of the Party, and the honest father who manages in his simplicity to see through the sham is again a dramatic enactment of Koestler's criticism of Communism. Wassilij's remark is a compact expression of Rubashov's more sophisticated criticism of Communism in the following chapter.

Koestler no doubt fashioned Rubashov's final speech as a parody of the Christian act of repentance and confession. Communism is like nothing so much as a religious movement - with its heaven in this world, with its own conceptions of the elect (the Party) and the damned (the counter-revolutionaries). Their god is "History," and his vicar the Party. Rubashov's feeling the need of being reconciled with the Party before his death is like the Christian's wish to die in the state of grace. This analogy helps to convey the psychological (indeed, the social-psychological) power of Communism and the Communist Party over those who give themselves to this movement.

In the 1930's the world was shaken to see prominent Bolsheviks confess to having been anti-Bolshevik (anti-Communist) traitors who connived to kill Stalin. This is what Koestler's book has set out to explain. From the point of view of an historical novel, Parts I, II, and III are Koestler's hypothesis, his rationalization of that actually happened. It is an hypothesis which very few thought of at the time.

The alternation of Biblical quotations muttered or thought by Wassilij with his daughter's readings from the paper makes a moving lyrical variation of the basic structure of the book: the oscillation between feeling and ideology. This chapter, in which Rubashov is only in the background, can stand as a compact analogue of the whole work.

CHAPTERS II-III

Back in his cell waiting for death Rubashov's old doubts about the Party reassert themselves with greater clarity and firmness than before. Even as he walks to his death in the execution cellar, he wonders if there is any point to the Party's existence. Something is wrong with reducing the individual to a fraction of the collective mass, with suppressing the impulses of the individual ego, with causing misery for the sake of getting rid of all misery, for the sake of a distant and abstract good.

> **Comment:** As indicated earlier, Rubashov's rationalization of No. 1's tyranny and his admission that he had been wrong to oppose it, are not strong enough entirely to quell the radical doubts he had when the novel opened. Koestler's fidelity to the emotional and intellectual complexity of the man here pays handsome dividends; for he is able to have the novel come full circle, to give the work a formal completeness. And simultaneously he is able to bring Rubashov's speculations to a climax by having Rubashov, after the exhaustion of the trial, accept at last openly and decisively the experience of the "oceanic sense" (Freud's name for mystical or religious or "transcendental" experience). The "grammatical fiction" becomes a reality for Rubashov in the last two chapters. Not that he is fully acquainted with it after all these years, but he accepts it and understands that it is wrong for the Party to try to suppress the core of the individual. And he is decisive in judging the Communist theory and practice fundamentally mistaken. Of course, he goes to his death still in confusion; Koestler will not transform him suddenly and unrealistically. But Rubashov does achieve the same clarity of insight Wassilij attained in (Part IV, Chapter I) and in almost the same words. All through the novel, the reader will recall, Rubashov had been trying to "work things out." This is his most "Communist" trait; it is what led him to "confess." And this is what Wassilij said (in so many words; the parallel can hardly be

accidental) it was dangerous to do. And now, in the most profound criticism of Communism in the whole novel - the climax of Koestler's judgment - Rubashov echoes Wassilij: the error has been "the running amuck of pure reason." Thus, after having previously justified the existence of "darkness at noon" Rubashov comes back to affirm its horrible and unjustifiable and confusing appearance as the climax of the work of "reason" (the Party). There has indeed been a logic at work in the events of the book, though it is not the logic that Rubashov had found earlier. His ineradicable self - his "I" - has managed to bore through the ideological wall into something approaching full consciousness. Though still at the moment of death beset with confusions, he has come a long way.

402 carries on a last comradely conversation with Rubashov. Rubashov had watched Harelip pass by in the corridor on the way to his death some minutes earlier. On the way to the execution cellar Rubashov's pince-nez falls off and breaks. Just as he is shot in the head, Rubashov's recurring nightmare of his arrest by the German secret police returns.

Comment: The breaking of Rubashov's pince-nez, a symbol of his self-possession, his individuality and his control, symbolizes the pathetic helplessness of the man as his public image and physical existence are destroyed by the - Party.

Koestler's obvious point in having Rubashov's nightmare of his Gestapo arrest and his execution by the Soviet secret police merge - in describing the pistol shot as a "blow" on the head - is that

the German National Socialist and the Soviet Communist regimes are quite analogous. The novel was completed at about the time of the signing of the Nazi-Communist pact, an historical symbol of the underlying similarity of the two regimes in which the individual is nothing.

DARKNESS AT NOON

CHARACTER ANALYSES

Nicolas Salmanovitch Rubashov

Rubashov is a concrete historical type - that is, he represents the "militant philosopher" of the mass movements of the twentieth century - specifically of Communism; but the Communist cadre, or member of the Party core, is merely the most extreme case of the intellectual apologist for a program for political action who is also the executor of that program. The main features of these secular missionary activists are their ruthless suppression of the individual and their adherence to ideological dogma.

Thus, Rubashov expends enormous effort trying to integrate his own fate into a social and political and national and historical vision of reality. Rubashov is more disturbed about what appear to be contradictions in the Party's actions and "History" than he is about his personal fate. The Communists are ruthless in carrying over into practical life all of the implications of a theory, regardless of consequences. Thus, Rubashov has been "consequent." And his sacrifice of Arlova because it was a "logical" thing to do is a prime locus of pathos in the novel. The description of life in Rubashov's country [the Soviet Union] is the prime example of the ruthless execution of theories regardless of their cost in human suffering. Unquestioning adherence to ideological dogma (which imparts a psychological security to the adherent) is the chief virtue which the militant-philosopher-priest-revolutionist must have if he is to put his policies in practice. Otherwise, he will falter; he will not be ruthless. In the course of the novel Rubashov loses both his "self-confidence" and his ruthlessness. That is why he is haunted almost from the opening page by the memory of Arlova. For in questioning his ideology, he is alienating himself from his "reality." He is torn by conflicting and contradictory emotions and, in the last analysis, cannot psychologically permit himself to acknowledge the enormity of his error - in adhering to a philosophy which is inherently unrealistic.

From a Communist point of view, the tragedy of the novel would consist in Rubashov's failure of will and intellect, his permitting "sentimentality" - pity, love, doubt - to get in the way of clear-cut ideology. From the non-Communist point of view the point of view of Koestler - Rubashov's tragedy consists in his inability to break out of his ideological prison: he goes to his death trying to make a last offering to the cause.

What distinguishes Rubashov from No. 1 - the dictator who is conducting the purge - is the fact that Rubashov has not managed completely to cut the "umbilical cord" which binds him to the "old world" - to the "pre-revolutionary" morality, to the tradition of parliamentary democracy. Hence his doubts about the - Party and his guilt. The conflict of moralities which is the **theme** of the book is dramatized by Rubashov's divided mind, which represents both the ideological and the non-ideological way of thinking.

Ivanov

The thematic function of Ivanov is to show us the ideological [Communist] mind which is imbued with all of Rubashov's principal attributes and yet is working on the other side in the doubt-ridden Rubashov's struggle with the Party. Ivanov and Rubashov could as easily have reversed their places if fate had taken different turns. Essentially, therefore, there is no difference between what goes on in Ivanov's mind and what goes on in Rubashov's. That is why Ivanov is the perfect interrogator of his old friend, and the reader can assume that the authorities knew exactly what they were doing when they chose him for the job. The arguments he makes are perfectly convincing to his former regimental commander because Ivanov's mind was schooled in the same ideology, the same practice, the same history. He differs somewhat from Rubashov in what Gletkin calls his cynicism - his willingness to treat the purge now going on as a game. It is reasonable to conclude that Ivanov would have tried to arrange things to get Rubashov off with his life as he promised. Aside from his sympathy for Rubashov and his desire to minimize his suffering, he does not appear to be touched by humanitarian impulses or by the "oceanic sense," which begin to dissolve Rubashov's ideology. But he teaches us just as much about the ideological mind, the Communist mind, as Rubashov does. And it is given to Ivanov to make the most comprehensive, the most rigorous summing-up of the Party's justification for all the horror and suffering it has caused (end of Part II). His "cynicism - that is, his knowledge that the political game is played for keeps, even with Party comrades, and his anti-Utopian attitudes (his conversation with Gletkin indicates that he does not completely believe that human nature is going to suffer a radical change under Socialism) and his Communist faith co-exist, perhaps uncomfortably, perhaps not, in his mind.

Gletkin

Gletkin is the spiritual son of Ivanov and Rubashov. This is not to imply that he matches them in intellectuality or sensitivity, but that they produced him, made him what he is - that is, he is what the Revolution needs at this moment. There is therefore a great **irony** in the confrontation between Gletkin and Rubashov that occupies the last third of the book. Father and son, the old and the new generations, confront each other across the table, with the old bending at last in service to the new - for that is the "logic" that the Fathers of the Revolution created. Unlike Rubashov, Gletkin (the "Neanderthal man") knows no doubts, is inhibited by none of the traditional virtues or sentiments. Unlike Ivanov and Rubashov, he has none of the finesse and subtlety of the older, conspiratorial, intellectual revolutionists. He is the veritable incarnation of the brutal regime of No. 1 [Stalin's U.S.S.R.] and, as Rubashov comes to admit, the perfect realization of the logic implicit in the Revolution itself. Gletkin is the walking repudiation of the ideology which created him: this is the man it makes. He can only be criticized from outside of the ideology, not within it, and once Rubashov convinces - himself that he has been wrong to yearn for a more democratic regime he can no longer scorn Gletkin's "wholesome sterility."

Gletkin's discussion of the peasants' built-in resistance to "progress" reveals the "logic" by which the Party rationalizes its brutal methods. Koestler's intent is to show that Gletkin is the Communist man par excellence of the Stalinist Era in the U.S.S.R. And if his dialectical skill may appear surprising at first sight, it is in reality merely the mechanical motions of a simple intellectual game.

No. 1:

No. 1 [Stalin] appears in only one scene - Rubashov's recollection of his quick departure from his country on a mission to Belgium. Yet his presence dominates the book, in the sense that No. 1 - himself and his policies - created the problems and generated the dilemma which is inflicting such pain in Rubashov. No. 1's rule is the pervasive "sickness" which makes Rubashov flee his country; it is the repression and the tyranny which make the more idealistic old Bolsheviks begin to oppose him - at least, in their minds and conversation. But just as Rubashov comes to admit that Gletkin is the logical result of the Party's ideology and practice, so also is No. 1. Every act of treachery and violence that Rubashov has "committed" is a comment on No. 1, as well as the Party. No. 1 stands for what the Party has become at this time in history, what the U.S.S.R. has become. And this is what creates all the problems for Rubashov and the other oppositionists. The book is about No. 1 as much as about anyone else. Described as reticent and ironic, he cultivates a kind of emperor-worship which serves to disarm the opposition and to consolidate his power.

One does not know that things would have turned out differently if Trotsky or Bukharin rather than Stalin had succeeded Lenin - probably not. But it must be emphasized that No. 1 is not described in the book as an alien phenomenon, something not essential to the practice of the Party's ideology. Rather, No. 1 is the "dialectical fulfillment" of the Party's development. Thus, though Rubashov begins his mental rebellion because of the mad tyranny of the regime in the Homeland of the Revolution and the total absence of democracy within the Party, he comes to see in the closing chapters that No. 1 is right and the opposition, wrong; therefore the root of the evil lies not merely in the person of this or that Party member or group, but in the ideology that the Party and No. 1 only attempt to put into practice.

Wassilij

He is one of the few non-Communist minds we encounter in the book, and therefore of great importance for purposes of contrast. The chief insurance against the ideologization of his mind has been his simple love and devotion for Rubashov - that is, the pre-eminence in his experience of human relations (something virtually excluded by Communist ideology) - and his Christianity (symbolized by the Bible he hides in his mattress) - that is, the form of expression of his "oceanic sense." The fact that he has a humble peasant's mentality should not prevent the reader from recognizing his thematic importance as a kind of norm of reality. He possesses those very qualities which Rubashov - especially in the last two chapters - comes to see that the Party has tragically repressed; and without these internal checks, the mind, "trying to figure things out," may be translated into the monstrosity of the Party, the U.S.S.R., and the principle that the end justifies the means. It is therefore of the highest significance to understand the parallelism between Wassilij's remarks in Part III, Chapter 1 and Rubashov's in Chapters II and III. There is another parallelism as well: Wassilij's signing the petition against Rubashov represents a kind of compromise of principle. But unlike Rubashov's denunciation of members of the opposition and of the innocent Arlova, Wassilij's signing can do no positive harm: it will only protect him from harassment and worse. Nevertheless, this is what people like Wassilij are reduced to in Communist society: they must conceal their religion, their personal loyalties; they must live in fear of losing bed and board, they must suffer being spied on by their children. Unlike Richard, Little Loewy, and the dockworkers, who were

Party members betrayed by the Party, Wassilij represents the so-called "masses," many of whom like Wassilij fought for the Revolution in the civil war, whose naive faith in the Party's promises have been betrayed by the Party. He is the surest proof that the Revolution has been a failure and the Party a fraud.

Wassilij's Daughter (Vera Wassiljovna)

Like her father, her function in the novel, is to represent the ordinary citizen, in her case the urban factory worker, so that we can see what Communist society does to the people. Of course, the country of the Party has no monopoly on filial infidelity, narrow-mindedness, gullibility, stupidity, insensitiveness, greed or cruelty. The point is that the Party, and the society it made, encourages this kind of behavior. It would be an act of "socialist virtue" for her to report a father for reactionary or oppositional opinions. Her stealing her father's Bible indicates the extent of her pettiness. The Party's policies, therefore, help to corrupt the corruptible, and in a particularly extreme way.

Arlova

As the only other woman in the novel beside Wassilij's daughter, comparisons between them inevitably arise. The salient difference is that Arlova gives no evidence that her basic womanliness has been invaded and dissipated by "masculine" ideology. Though not a Communist in a "cadre" sense (as a member of a delegation abroad she comes under Party discipline, and is subject to formal "criticism" at a "cell" meeting, but there is no indication that she is even a candidate member of the Party) she is employed by an important State department and even charged with maintaining the legation library. Her life is therefore closely tied to the Party. It might be proper to say then that she may be set beside Wassilij as another "non-Communist mind" in the novel. With her, personal relations are all, and her power over Rubashov's memory and feelings signifies the rekindling of personal affections over the glacial force of ideology. The reader should note that she is not properly a member of the opposition; she is therefore completely innocent - even by the "logic" which convinces Rubashov that he has been guilty - of oppositional activities. That makes Rubashov's sacrifice of her all the more dishonorable. The others - the men from the photograph, the former members of the Central Committee of the Party - like Rubashov were at least playing the game and lost. But the sacrifice of Arlova is quite acceptable to the morality of the Party, which is Rubashov's morality. That she was his mistress, that he loved her, only serves to show how uncompromising the Party ideology can be. Koestler is no doubt also underscoring the psychotic suspicion and paranoia which can justify the trial and execution of someone because her brother is married to a foreigner. The motive for her sacrifice is probably a compound of neurotic suspicion and handy expediency. It is useful to show "common" people that even one so lowly as a young secretary can be an enemy of the State. But Arlova, as devoted and meek and pitiable as a dumb beast, patiently suffers whatever Rubashov will do with her. Her character is never fully explored by Koestler, who is primarily interested in her significance for Rubashov and for the regime.

Little Loewy

Little Loewy has many functions in the novel. Through him we get a picture of the Party as it operates outside of the "Fatherland of the Revolution," thereby extending the scope and interest of the novel. The nature and power of the Party is more fully revealed because of this - the Party functions in its international relations with the same callous expediency as it is wont to use at home. Loewy is also one of the more important examples of how the Party pays its own most devoted and most talented members with ingratitude and deceit. Since he is one of those characters who has had certain doubts of a "technical" and ah ethical nature about the Party, Loewy thus gives corroboration to Rubashov's own doubts, and, through his life story and principled rejection of the Party's duplicity, he helps to instruct and influence Rubashov's own "rebellion." Further, the difficulties he had being reintegrated into - the Party show the Party's inefficiency, induced by suspicion and endemic fear. Finally, the rebellion he leads is the most self-conscious and complete "break" with the Party we encounter in the book - for he knows what refusal to obey a command will mean. Little Loewy has another function as well; he offers an example of the hold the Party has over its devotees. Like Rubashov and Richard and so many others he can envision no concrete alternative; that is, his disillusion drives him to despair, to suicide - rather than to another mode of life, another social and political commitment. More than Richard, he shows the self-destruction that membership in the Party inevitably involves: suppression of the individual ego first; and, in many cases, self-assertion is followed only by suicide.

Richard

Richard lacks the sophistication of Loewy. At nineteen he represents the unspoiled idealism of the youthful novitiate. His fate is thus all the more touching. The flower of the Party is crushed, destroyed, turned over to its enemies. Therefore, though he was not (by Party logic) innocent, turning Richard over to the Gestapo is one of the most despicable official - acts Rubashov has to perform. Richard had proposed to show how the Party is at war with social reality, turns political crises to its own advantage and is at the service of no general humanity. Again, Rubashov is instructed and influenced.

Bogrov

On one side of Rubashov is the Communist mind that chooses to "die in silence." He is the man who believes he is right, that No. 1 is wrong, and, presumably, that ideological correctness justifies refusing to cooperate in serving the purposes of his accuser and executioner. Bogrov's rebellion is not against the ideology of Communism or its incarnation, the Party, rather it is against those who, he thinks, have perverted its purposes. In standing up under torture until death in the execution cellar he is dying for both principle and honor. One may conjecture that had he had Rubashov's subtle mind, he would have been open to the same kind of ideological appeals which worked on Rubashov. But Bogrov is not a "militant philosopher"; he is rather the ideologically informed soldier (in his case, Admiral of the Fleet) who can only honestly and forthrightly do his duty as he sees fit. He is one of those who believe in immediate promotion of world revolution. Bogrov, too, is one of the many people devoted to Rubashov. Observe that in refusing to die in silence, in agreeing to aid his executioner, Rubashov is betraying Bogrov as well as the others. Bogrov dies as a way of demonstrating the values of the Party which can sentence a man to death for recommending the "wrong" armament policy. Bogrov takes his place with Richard and Little Loewy as another variation in the Party/member relationship.

406

On the other side of Rubashov is 406, who responds to the brutal tyranny and failure of the Party in the Homeland of the Revolution by going insane. With 406 Koestler brings yet another type of the Party faithful into the picture: the devotee who was never really an activist, a rather harmless professor, who worshipped the Party with a childlike simplicity. His refuge in insanity indicates both the depth of his faith - he could not bear disillusion - and the utter disparity between the Communistic promise and the poverty of its fulfillment. This is the **irony** in 406's insistence that he has come to the wrong country by mistake. Like Bogrov and the others, 406 is an example to Rubashov, and a rebuke to him, the Party and the ideology of Communism. The story of his life as 402 relates it to Rubashov helps the reader to understand the apocalyptic meaning that Communism and the Soviet Union had for so many in the twenties and thirties.

Harelip

One may assume that Harelip was never really a member of the opposition - passive though that was - that it was his father's opposition which has made him suspect and a prisoner. Harelip compliments Rubashov in this novelistic representation of the Purge trials, in that his confession was the result of torture. This is another explanation for the public confessions, though Koestler does not emphasize this because it was an obvious hypothesis and his explanation of Rubashov's motive was original. Harelip's "use" by the State is, like that of the innocent Arlova, a heinous example of the principle that human beings may be tortured, abused and executed merely in order to aid the Party's domestic propaganda.

Professor Kieffer

Rubashov's old friend and the friend of the "old man" represents the opposition who believed that No. 1 had betrayed the principles of the Revolution. His naive belief that the Party would eventually depose No. 1 shows that he misunderstood the significance of No. 1 and the real nature of the Party. Kieffer's existence proves that there was an opposition, however ineffectual. There is an ironic lesson in Kieffer's complaint about the lack of democracy; Kieffer surely participated in all the violence and bloodshed that brought the Party to power. Koestler may be suggesting that the total abandonment of traditional ethical restraints can never serve as the establishment of a humane regime.

Paul

Since he is not nearly as intelligent, sophisticated and talented as Little Loewy, Paul serves to represent the ordinary workers. His reaction to the Party's betrayal of its professed principles is decisive because he has not cut out common sense as have his more "sophisticated" Party colleagues.

Bill

Bill is a writer; his disappointment at the Soviet Union's trading with the Fascists no doubt represents the view of many intellectuals who seemed to see in the U.S.S.R. a country whose idealism would permit it to rise above "power politics."

The Men In The Photograph

The photograph of the delegates to the first Congress of the Communist Party of the U.S.S.R. becomes an important symbol in the book. The picture includes men like No. 1, who would put many of his colleagues to death for the sake of his own power and the triumph of his policy. It includes those like Rubashov who did not have the stomach for No. 1's ruthless measures. It includes those like the "old man" who died before the Party began to slaughter its own as well as others. The disappearance of the picture from the walls of innumerable rooms in the Homeland of the Revolution is a symbol of the instability of the Party's life.

The Old Man

Lenin never appears in the novel except in memory and in the famous photograph of the delegates to the First Party Congress. His figure symbolizes that era before, during, and after the Revolution when the "running amuck of pure reason" was not so visible to members of the Party. They had to wait for Stalin to see the logical implications of the revolution. Lenin did not tolerate Party opposition any more than his successor; however, his methods of dealing with it were persuasion, exile and imprisonment instead of execution and assassination. But, Lenin, who died in 1924, had gained power by seizing the government from the Democratic Socialists, who were more or less in the tradition of Western parliamentarism and who would have shrunk from the ruthless violence and destruction of Lenin's Communist Party.

Amy

Richard's seventeen-year-old wife stands as doubly symbolic of the Party's betrayal. It is probable that she was betrayed to the Gestapo by Richard's good friend and her lover, the cinema operator.

The Peasant

The peasant is one of the four or five non-Communists in the novel (the others are Wassilij, Arlova, 402 and, possibly, Harelip). The peasant's story of how he came to be confined as a "reactionary" indicates the profound resistance to collectivization and modernization which to this day makes the peasants such a problem for all Communist countries. The peasant's description of the idyllic sheepherding scene indicates his non-ideological way of viewing reality. It is also a fleeting image of repose, of an existence apart from the ideological treadmill, close to a basic reality (cf. Rubashov's dream, Question 2).

402

As one of the only two "genuine counterrevolutionists" in the novel 402 has a special interest for the reader. Koestler could not have found a more anti-Bolshevik character than a Czarist officer. Although he cannot possibly participate in the debates because he is not even an intellectual let alone a Communist,

402's role is relevant to the main themes of the book. In the first place he has been sentenced for thirty years to an isolation cell - with no exercise permitted. Under Czarism, imprisoned Socialist revolutionists were often placed in camps in Siberia where they were able to write books advocating Socialism. And though he is a "nonpolitical" man, he carries in him the old-fashioned notions of virtue: Koestler is therefore able to confront in a radical way, through the conversations between Rubashov and 402, the diametrically opposed notions of honor, hence of human conduct, which were at stake in the civil war and the Communist Revolution. Thus, 402 is eminently impractical, romantic; Rubashov, ruthlessly practical (in his Communist ideology). On the level of intellect there can be no communication between them. But when Rubashov is moved by extra-ideological considerations, his feeling, his sense of the "invisible writing," is something 402 would thoroughly understand. As one of the non-Communists in the novel, 402 presents one of many possible challenges to the regime. Further, the successful human relationship between 402 and Rubashov is an implicit rebuke to the ideology which sees such things as irrelevant, at best. 402's interest in women and jokes, seems to fit in with a kind of stereotype of the Czarist officer that Rubashov (and Koestler) model him on.

The Grammatical Fiction

The personal pronoun "I" is "grammatical fiction" because, according to Communist ideology, man's existence is totally social. One thinks in the collective, one acts in the collective. The Party, not the person, is the supreme entity for the Communist. Thus, the notion that there is a radical, autonomous individuality is a "fiction." The individual person is merely equal to the quantity one, is just a part of the larger whole. He has none of that sacredness which Western tradition will grant him, even over the collective. Therefore, Rubashov speaks of his own self-assertive ego as if it were another character who has invaded his mind to do battle against him; for Rubashov is habituated to being entirely a participant in the life of the Party. The Grammatical Fiction, then, represents that part of Rubashov's spirit which has managed to survive the ravages of ideology. Koestler's point is that the most elementary, and at the same the most humane and noble, of men's impulses is systematically and self-consciously extirpated by Communism. It is the coexistence in his mind of collectivist ideology and the "I" that makes Rubashov's life such a tormenting confusion.

Minor Characters

Herr von Z.; the stenographer; the doctor; the barber; the warder.

DARKNESS AT NOON

GENERAL COMMENTARY

PHYSICAL STRUCTURE - PLOT

On the surface, the novel is divided into parts according to the stages of Rubashov's argument with himself. Thus, the first hearing (Part I) is the preliminary probing of the argument, the second hearing the **climax** and decision, the third hearing (Part III) the confirming **denouement**, and The Grammatical Fiction (Part IV) a postscript reconsideration of the argument, pointing in a quite different direction from Rubashov's diary notes.

Actually, the basic organization of the novel is twofold, in imitation of the oscillating nature of the action. Thus, the movement of the book turns on the decision at the end of Part II which is virtually in the physical center of the novel. The suspense consists first in waiting for this decision and then in waiting for its full implications to be revealed.

This twofold structure is seen also in the past/present alternation of scenes. The present of Rubashov's arrest and interrogation is played against the past of the flashbacks - reveries, daydreams, meditations - and reports and conversations about the past. Again, physical form is in imitation of thematic action; for what is at stake in the present is colored by the issues which emerge from the past, as Rubashov moves from one side of his mind to the other.

Darkness at Noon is a novel of ideas (as are all of Koestler's novels). Yet, Koestler has taken pains to exploit the emotional drama inherent in the setting of the novel. The basic situation is charged with suspense, excitement and shock. Rubashov's highly abstract meditations and conversations are weighted with the pathos of a man facing his imminent death - to say nothing of the enormous emotional investment he has in the intellectual problems. Plot and setting have all the emotional power of a horror film. There is first of all the basic situation of a man waiting for his death - of men waiting for their death in isolation cells, under harassment and torture; with spyholes in the doors of their narrow cells. There is the interrogation and the blinding glare of bright lights and the haze of sleepless nights. There is the terrible apparatus of the execution: advance warning of the execution party through the prisoners' communication system (the quadratic alphabet); the final conversation with one's neighbor (of months, weeks, or days); the banging on the doors - the prisoners' drum roll of solidarity, release, protest, which accompanies the execution ceremony; the reading of the sentence to the prisoner in the cell; the rough, impersonal binding of hands behind the back; the march down the corridor under the eyes of fellow prisoners getting a preview of their own end; the uncomfortable descent down the winding steel stairs to the execution cellar; the condemned's last few seconds of thought walking ahead of his executioner, who finally delivers the "blow" in the neck and, then, the coup de grace. And in Rubashov's case, he has seen and heard Harelip's procession just a few minutes before! Thus, the "extremism" of the intellectual subject is modified by an extremism of nervous suspense. The melodrama of the novel, of course, merely reflects the reality of the Communist Party.

THEMATIC STRUCTURE

The Conflict Of Moralities: The basic **theme** of *Darkness at Noon* is the confrontation of moralities - the morality of individual dignity and benevolence and the morality of collectivism and expediency. This is what lends the novel its universality beyond the "contemporary" relevance of Communism; for, in one form or another, this conflict between absolute ethical rules and utilitarian expediency is perennial. The social and political revolution which is the immediate subject of the book is, in essence, Koestler claims, a revolution in ethics. Traditional Western ethics, to which our society continues to pay lip-service at least, relates every free choice to a norm, a human image or nature, capable of actualization in the present. The ethics of Communism scorns the paltry humanity of the present for the sake of a human image that can only be actualized in the future. Traditional ethics regards the individual as a being unto himself with rights held to be sacrosanct. Communist ethics accords this sacredness only to the collective - to the Party, which is progressively realizing Communist society. Therefore: for the traditional ethician the end (purpose) of an activity cannot justify all means, because some means violate his image of man: there are some absolute do's and don't's, regardless of the goodness of the end in view. For the Communist ethician no given human act can, in itself, violate his image of man, because a proper humanity will not exist until Communism is realized: there is only one absolute do/don't which determines the rightness of human action - the end of achieving Communism. Traditional ethics is rooted in the inherent worth of the individual;

Communist ethics is rooted in the collective obedience to the will of "History."

The oceanic sense (a term which Koestler took from Freud, who used it to indicate man's religious or mystical faculty) puts men in touch with human solidarity, enables them to sense the essential humanity in other living men; it is the impulse to charity, to obedience to, for example, the Ten Commandments. This "oceanic sense" - a check on "reason" - is one with the "Grammatical Fiction," the free individual identity which the Party collective would stifle. "Reason," as Koestler uses the concept, is not rationality, but reason "run amuck," reason divorced from reality. Thus, as Koestler presents it, ideology- "reason" - follows the logic of an idea; the Grammatical Fiction seeks the logic of reality. In fact, it is necessary (in Part IV) for the "oceanic sense" to be released in order for Rubashov to see the logical contradictions of his ideology! The intensity of *Darkness at Noon* results from the continual clash of reality ("oceanic sense," Grammatical Fiction) and ideology.

The dramatic expression of this thematic structure may be discussed under five chief headings: Ends and Means; the Individual and the Collective; the meaning of Honor; the importance of Personal Relations; Pity and Power.

The concrete circumstances which give rise to the moral problems Rubashov faces can be summarized by asking if the achievement of the good justifies any action. The question forces itself on him for two reasons: 1) the good which has been sought is nowhere in sight; 2) his still vital "oceanic sense" repudiates his ideology of ruthless expediency. Here, the innocence of the victims of Rubashov's action (Richard, Loewy, Arlova) and of No. 1's action (the suffering subjects of the "Homeland of the Revolution" and the defendants in the show-trials) is what makes the question of the end justifying any means so urgent, so difficult, so traumatic for Rubashov.

The inherent worth and dignity of the idealistic victims of the Party as well as the self-assertion of the individual personality (the Grammatical Fiction), cry out against anonymous submergence in the cruel collective of the Party - where a man is merely the "quotient of one million divided by one million." The subjects of the flashbacks and Rubashov's (newly discovered) "I" seem to claim a value which transcends their "use" to the Party.

The debate about honor between 402 and Rubashov poses the central question of the novel in yet another way. For 402, honor is linked to the intuitions of the "oceanic sense" (however crudely 402 may state it). For Rubashov and the Communists, honor is tied to usefulness to the Party. But Rubashov's deep guilt for his (and the Party's) past deeds gives the lie to his glib "logic."

The challenge to ideology is again forced by the emotional pull of personal relations. The devotion of Bogrov, the completely generous love of Arlova, the dependence of Richard, the trust of Loewy - all of these murdered for the convenience of the Party - claim from Rubashov a loyalty which his ideology scorns.

Finally, the power which the Party's ideology permits it to wield ruthlessly is challenged by Rubashov's natural compassion for the suffering "masses" who must live and die for an abstraction called "mankind."

With variant repetition Koestler opposes the two moralities. The contrast can only prove to the reader that the one is a basic human necessity, the other, a grotesque inversion of all morality.

ACTION

Reality Vs. Ideology: Virtually all of the action of the novel is mental. The incidents in the novel intrude upon Rubashov's ideological consciousness and disturb his ideological peace. Throughout he is engaged in straining against the shackles of ideological dogma; the Grammatical Fiction fights a subtle and devious war with [Communist] ideology, which has claimed right of possession over Rubashov's mind. From the time he sees the stick - like arms of 407 until just before the end Rubashov swings from one alternative to the other. Even after he decides to "capitulate," he continues to feel the tug of the old scruples and doubts. The movement of the book is that of a pendulum; only, the oscillation between the poles of reality and ideology is jerky, pained, urgent, sometimes frantic. This oscillating movement is characteristic of the mind in doubt before two alternatives. In this case the pathos derives from the fact that the stakes are spiritual life and death.

The question which this action poses, then, is this: Is Rubashov's mind so rotted with the corruption of ideology that he will deny the reality the deepest springs of his identity cry out for him to affirm? Will the accent of Koestler's work be on human failure and will ideology win? Or will it be on human triumph and will ideology lose?

Ideology, of course, wins; it has too deeply eaten into Rubashov's consciousness; he cannot overthrow the habit of a lifetime. But, after he has given "logic" its due, he moves (once again, and for the last time) to the other alternative. His last meditation, after having paid his debt both to ideology and to his guilt, gives free rein to the "oceanic sense," and he makes a bold, profound intuitive critique of ideology and of "reason run amuck." And this aspect to the tragic finale is consistent with the nature of the struggle the book has dramatized. Both forces in Rubashov's nature are too strong for either to be completely stifled. The "relaxation" that follows the perverted ideological self-abasement of the confession and trial permits a free flow of feeling, and Rubashov is able to respond to the emotions which spoke to him in the arms of the Pieta, in Bogrov's last cry, in Arlova's love, and in all the dreams and memories that cluster around the non-ideological "I."

Darkness at Noon shows us the ideological mind in action; in the various characters it presents a kind of anatomy of the ideological mind. The book is not about Rubashov merely: he is just the chief and most complex example. Most of the characters are united in an analogy of action; they are all doing the same thing, albeit in, a different way. For the unity of the novel consists in the histrionic knowledge we get of the ideological mind, and no single character can display fully all its twists and turns. Thus, the characters can be classified according to the way they cope with the exigencies of ideology. There are three groups of characters, three sets of analogous reactions to the ideological strain: 1) those who manage to break through the ideological wall; 2) those who try to break through, or at least question their ideology; 3) those who do not try at all, who have surrendered completely, whose thinking implicitly conforms to the ideological straitjacket. The characters are united by a common ideology [Communism] even as their different histories produce characteristic adaptations to this ideology. Finally, there is a fourth group: those completely outside the ideological world, who are united to the action by way of contrast or critique. The members of this last group are, in one way or another, in touch with reality, and therefore have affinities with those other characters who somehow manage to overcome ideology.

Thus, Richard and Loewy, in the final acts of their lives, rebel against the Party. Though their rebellion is not without ambiguity (Richard is broken by his excommunication from the Party and Loewy driven to suicide), in each there is a clear-sighted choice of reality over ideology.

Rubashov and, Koestler seems to imply, many of the (mental) opposition are only partly in touch with reality. They can only partially comprehend the chaos that ideology has produced. Whereas in Richard and Loewy the oscillating mind moves to the pole of reality, in Rubashov (and, presumably, many of his friends like Prof. Kieffer) there is mainly indecision and suspense. Rubashov touches both poles repeatedly in the novel. Because he does manage to throw off ideology at the end, after his crucial "logical" decision, he might well be placed with Loewy and Richard. At any rate, for complete Party men like Richard, Loewy, and Rubashov, there is no place else to go; their final rejections of ideology have the quality of a postscript to an already spent existence. Rubashov, however, does not actually rebel or refuse to cooperate with the Party. In addition to the show-trial defendants and the opposition, 406 also belongs to the divided minds. He was able to perceive the chaos the Party has made when he came to the U.S.S.R. And so torn was his mind by this honest confrontation of ideology, that he sought the peace of insanity.

In the third group we find Ivanov, Gletkin, No. 1, Wassilij's daughter, and Bogrov. Gletkin and No. 1 have not the slightest doubt. They are completely given up to "Historical Necessity." They have fully rooted out any vestiges of a "bourgeois" past. They and Wassilij's daughter seem ideological robots. They need not suffer the torment of the oscillating mind. For them, reality is transformed by ideology. Ivanov is also fully ideologized, but he seems to have retained subtle pre-ideological traces which makes Gletkin's instigation of his murder appropriate. Bogrov's rebellion, as far as we know, is not against ideology but against those persons who imprison, torture, and, finally, murder him.

In 402, Wassilij and Arlova, we see a free, though partial, affirmation and recognition of reality, because they are not burdened; with ideological shutters. 402 retains the essential idealism attached to the notion of honor and warm human relations. Wassilij and Arlova are capable of sincere love of other human beings. Wassilij is able to see "thinking things out too much" as a great heresy of the mind, a flight from reality. These characters, in the simplicity of their affection and thought, offer an imperishable rebuke to the ideological mind.

The fatality of this mind, as exhibited in all of the ideologues, is that it blocks off those avenues to any part of reality which will contradict its premises. The result is that ideology is full of contradictions! This is Rubashov's torment and his fate. He is swept by two irreconcilable forces; and his habit of making sense of things dooms him to the circle of ideology - makes confession (as Ivanov astutely sees) inevitable. In the more consistent ideologues, of course, like No. 1 and Gletkin, any contact with reality results in human destruction.

VIRTUES AND LIMITATIONS

The great strength of *Darkness at Noon* is its fidelity to its subject: the mind caught in the tangles of ideology, yet feeling those human impulses which contradict ideology because they are antecedent to any ideology. To anyone who has lived in the second quarter of the twentieth century Rubashov's character must seem marvelously real - and this in spite of the fact that it is so removed from the experience of ordinary minds. To read

Darkness at Noon is to have the sensation of watching some strange perversion which is nonetheless credible. Rubashov's distorted personality, possessed by an ideology which renders him practically insane, is yet somehow familiar to persons of our time and place, recognizable. And the freedom and complexity that he retains permits all the other wooden figures in the novel to be taken seriously also. By the time Rubashov makes his fated decision, the reader accepts it as a faithful representation of a probable reality. Nor are the intimations of his "oceanic sense" any less convincing than the intellectual tyranny of ideology. Reality makes an end-run around ideological defenses and touches Rubashov without his knowing it. His eyes are drawn to the Pieta in the Bavarian museum because he is feeling an unconscious pity for Richard (indeed, pity for others is the dominant emotion challenging "reason's" ideology). And, as indicated above, Koestler makes excellent use of the melodramatic setting of the novel. He also has a firm command of Communist dialectic, something that very few non-Communist novelists could claim, which is essential to the "**realism**" of *Darkness at Noon*.

Yet with all this, there is a certain narrowness in the incessant oscillation of this novel. If Dostoevsky is Koestler's predecessor here, *Darkness at Noon* would only make a portion of one of Dostoevsky's great anatomies of human experience. There is, for example, in Koestler's work no intellect matching Rubashov's which can serve as a norm of sanity and rationality. The religious point of view is represented admirably - but incompletely - in Wassilij. There is no one in the novel who has broken with Communism completely and wishes to fight it for what it is. Nor is there a conservative, or democrat, or liberal, or socialist, or republican. There are, further, no variations of ideological rationalism; only Communism is shown. These many exclusions, of course, made Koestler's novelistic task easier, and what he lost in breadth of experience he somewhat gained in intensity. But the result is a much narrower work, a less complete experience. The perverted rationalism that is ideology - and is the universal subject of the book - becomes submerged in the example of Communism. Thus, while it is undoubtedly true that the book is a marvelous revelation of the Communist ideology and the Communist mind, the essential and perennial temptation of reason and will to defy reality is somewhat obscured by the hyper-presence of the particular case.

Koestler's ambitions, unfortunately, did not require him to explore the psychological roots of this ideology, the motivation to "tear the skin off mankind and give him a new one." This is a loss to the reader's full exploration of the experience presented, as is the author's decision (inevitable under the limitations he accepted) not to follow up his hints about the "dangers of reason" with a fuller analysis. With a subject of such strangeness, the need for some representation of a norm of reality also becomes greater. Koestler, however, decided to stay very close to the original historical events which occasioned his book in the first place, and within his original intention, sensuous form and thematic content are perfectly wedded.

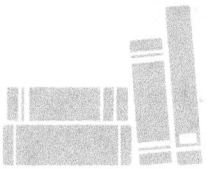

DARKNESS AT NOON

ESSAY QUESTIONS AND ANSWERS

Question: What is the significance of the title?

Answer: The words "darkness at noon" are a contraction of a line from Milton's dramatic poem *Samson Agonistes*: the full line spoken by the blinded Samson reads, "Dark, dark, dark, amid the blaze of noon." In Koestler's novel the blaze of noon is the triumph of the Communist Revolution on an area one-sixth the land surface of the earth. "Reason" has plumbed the laws of "History," and has organized a Party to carry out the commands of "History." To a Communist, the Revolution is the noon of "History," the turning point in time. When Communism succeeds the sun of "History" will have set - for the goal (end) of "History" will have been reached. But the actual fruit of the Revolution and of Party activity around the world has been an enormous increase in human suffering and in the politics of deceit, hypocrisy, and violence. By any sane standard the ideology and its agent, the Party, have been a gross failure. This contradiction between promise and fulfillment, pretense and actuality, ideology and reality is the meaning of the contrast darkness at noon. This is the contradiction which invades Rubashov's consciousness (and that of his comrades, Richard and Loewy) and causes him such anguish. The **irony** that the most radical - the most "consequent" - attempt to model society according to the schemes of "reason" ends in such "great darkness" is Koestler's comment on Communism and on all such attempts to ignore the intimations of the oceanic sense.

Question: What is the significance of Rubashov's dreams?

Answer: Rubashov has four significant dreams: the dream of his arrest by the German National Socialist Secret Police (Gestapo); his dream of Richard; of Little Loewy; and of the scene of the poplars, blue sky, white cloud and landscape of his father's estate where he passed his childhood. The first dream is obviously a nightmare based on the terrifying experience of his arrest in Germany. It indicates the kind of latent fear that an agent of the Party must support. But this first dream becomes an ironic comment on the Homeland of the Party; for conditions are no different there than under the German Dictatorship. This nightmare frames the novel; by the time it recurs at the end, confused in Rubashov's mind with the reality of his own country, the novel has fully worked out the parallel that was implicit in the second chapter. Rubashov's dreams of Richard and Loewy suggest his unconscious guilt - guilt that the hard-core Party member would not admit - for the Party's hypocrisy and treachery, of which he has been an effective agent. But Rubashov's fourth dream has nothing immediately to do with the Party, his ideology, or his current situation. When, towards the end of the novel (Part IV), Rubashov consciously recalls this boyhood scene he is able to recognize that it evokes the "oceanic state" - during which he can sense that there is a measure transcending that of reason," in which he breaks the Party rules about suppressing the "I," the radical and unique individuality of the person which is the source and ground of the ethics the Party calls "bourgeois" and "sentimental." When the dream of his childhood occurs - in the midst of his interrogation by Gletkin - he is making an unconscious declaration that his "capitulation" to the Party is not complete. This scene from Rubashov's childhood, from his pre-Party life, is especially appropriate because it indicates the source of his doubts about his ideology. When he was converted to the Communist ideology, apparently he was unable to extirpate all the premises he accepted in his childhood. Finally, this idyllic scene - so calm and peaceful - has a relation to the incessant oscillation between doubt (about the Party) and faith (in the Party). It represents that circle of repose, that place of rest, that has been denied Rubashov both in his present situation and in the life of frenzied activity he has led in the service of his ideology.

Question: Discuss the **theme** of "payment" in the novel.

Answer: Throughout the first part of the novel Rubashov is haunted by the notion that he must pay for the betrayals that he has made in the Party's name. This idea is a principal manifestation of his sense of guilt. But the **theme** quickly becomes more complicated as the reader discovers that he must "pay" for Arlova as well. She was not betrayed on order of the Party as were Richard and Loewy; rather Rubashov swore that she was an "oppositionist" in order to save himself from closer scrutiny. A third category of those to whom Rubashov owes "payment" includes persons such as 402, who were "objectively" enemies of the Party, of progress. Rubashov's "mystical" reading of "the invisible writing" tells him that he must also "pay" for whatever he did to fight the real enemies of the Party and bring the Revolution into being. Finally, as a fourth variation on the theme, Rubashov realizes, while theorizing in his diary, that, as a member of the opposition - though only in thought - he must "pay" for having mis-read "History" and not seeing that No. 1's totalitarian policies were necessary. Thus, Rubashov has four different sources of guilt -

three appealing to his non-or pre-ideological self, and one to his ideological conscience: 1) official guilt - for what he did as an officer of the Party; 2) personal guilt - for what he did to save himself; 3) historical guilt - for what he did to the "necessary" casualties of the Revolution; 4) Party or ideological guilt - for having been "objectively" counterrevolutionary. Although Rubashov makes his decision to confess explicitly in order to "pay," to expiate his crimes against the Party, he also manages to assuage his more human guilt for having betrayed and sent to their death fellow human beings and for, like his comrades in the Party, having wrought so much human suffering for the sake of the "super-humanity to come." This simultaneous, multiple "payment," in his acceptance of an ignoble and perverse abasement, in embracing his tyrant executioner and seeing his reputation utterly besmirched by a monstrous lie, may perhaps explain the intellectual and imaginative freedom which he experiences in the last two chapters of the book. Of course, *Darkness at Noon* is also about the price that the mind pays for surrendering itself to ideology. This is Rubashov's tragic failure. He spends most of his time trying to figure things out but is reduced to being torn by conflicting emotions. Rubashov becomes aware of his sense of "payment" only in the closing pages of the novel.

Question: If *Darkness at Noon* is such a faithful representation of the Communist point of view, how can the reader be sure where the author stands?

Answer: Because Koestler presents Ivanov's and Gletkin's arguments so forcefully, and because Rubashov's theory of the "relative maturity of the masses" seems to be a thorough justification for the regime of the U.S.S.R., some readers have claimed that the book could be a justification of rather than an attack on Communism. John Atkins remarks that "the usual characterization of *Darkness at Noon* as a full-blooded attack on Communism is a travesty" (Arthur Koestler, p. 180). It is nevertheless indubitable that Koestler is intentionally revealing Communism to be a horrible perversion of human thought and action. It must first of all be seen that the English public, to whom the book was first presented in 1941, could only ratify this judgment, because the Communist mind as revealed in the book flouted most brutally all their political and moral preconceptions. The author knew this, and he made no attempt to forestall this judgment. After all, the portrayal of traditional ethics is presented most sympathetically in the book. Richard, Little Loewy and the dockworkers are all appealing characters. The only Communist other than Rubashov who is likeable is put to death for no good reason other than Gletkin's fear of him. The contrast between the Christian Wassilij and his Communist daughter cannot but show to the former's advantage. And Koestler has placed this scene in the strategic final part of the novel. The most obvious indication of the author's outlook is the rebuttal to Ivanov's and Gletkin's and Rubashov's rationalizations which Rubashov makes in the last two chapters of the book. Not only has Koestler given the last word to the Grammatical Fiction, he has Rubashov make a more profound analysis of the root error of Communism than previously. Finally, the parallel between the German National Socialist and the Communist regimes is reaffirmed in the closing lines in the book. Even those persons who are alienated from the traditional morality and politics of the West would therefore have to recognize that Koestler has so organized his novel as to lead the reader to sympathize with Rubashov's oceanic sense against ideology. Finally, Communists have unanimously condemned the novel and feared it as a powerful weapon.

SUGGESTED ESSAY TOPICS

Each of the four parts of *Darkness at Noon*, as well as the novel as a whole is headed by epigraphs - quotations from various authors. Show how each epigraph summarizes an important **theme** in the book.

In the conversation between Ivanov and Rubashov at the end of Part II, Dostoevsky's *Crime and Punishment* is discussed. Show how Dostoevsky and Koestler are treating a very similar **theme**. What is the chief difference between Dostoevsky's presentation of the ends-and-means **theme** and Koestler's?

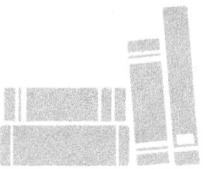

AGE OF LONGING

TEXTUAL ANALYSIS

PART I

....

Fedya Grigoryevitch Nikitin is the grandson of an Armenian grandfather (Arin) and a Georgian grandmother (Tamar). Arin worked in the shoe shop of Niko, Tamar's father, in Tiflis, the capital of Georgia. Both old men were nationalist revolutionists, atheists, and materialists, and both were uneducated and illiterate. Gregor Nikitin, a member of the Communist Party and later a hero of the Communist Revolution, married Arin's daughter (also named Tamar). Fedya Nikitin was born in 1912 in the oil town of Baku, in Azerbaidzhan. Georgia, Armenia and Azerbaidzhan were non-Russian countries in the Russian Empire. After the Communist Revolution they declared their independence, but were forcibly integrated into the Communist Empire (the Soviet Union). It is not certain, but it is probable that Gregor (Grisha) is at least partly Russian. Gregor played an important part in the Revolution and was captured by counterrevolutionary troops during the subsequent civil war. He has passed on to his son his quasi-religious faith in the Utopian promises of Communism. After Fedya's mother died, his grandfather Arin came to Baku and took his grandson to Moscow where he was extremely well-treated and educated as the son of the legendary hero of the Revolution, Gregor Nikitin.

Fedya was thoroughly indoctrinated in the ideology of Communism and was taught to suppress every human instinct for the sake of Party discipline. When his individualistic adolescent mistress (Nadeshda) came under suspicion of undermining the Communist youth movement, his schoolboy ideological zeal forced him first to convince himself and then to inform the State Security office that she was an active "counterrevolutionary" - an act which caused his interrogator, Maximov, to mark him out for service in the State Security (secret police).

He is now (19-) in his early forties, a cultural attaché to the Russian embassy in Paris. Actually, he is still working for the secret police, preparing lists of those Frenchmen who will have to be executed or imprisoned (in order to eliminate any potential resistance when the French Communist Party, backed by the military power of the U.S.S.R., assumes power in France and requests to be incorporated into the Soviet State.)

Hydie Anderson is the daughter of an alcoholic mother (Julia) who had to be placed in a sanitarium when Hydie was fifteen and of a member of the United States Army, Colonel Anderson. After her mother was put away Hydie was sent to a convent school in England run by her aunt, a Mother Superior of the Roman Catholic Order of the Holy Virgin. While at school Hydie became a devout Catholic. She developed a schoolgirl crush on one of the nuns, Sister Boutillot, who repulsed her with the dogma and doctrine of the church. Hydie had already taken her first vows, preliminary to being inducted into the Order as a nun, when the sight of soldiers mutilated in the second World War and the painful death of a very young student at the school caused her to lose her Catholic, Christian faith. She left the convent to get married at the age of nineteen, but was soon divorced from her sexually unsatisfying husband.

Hydie is now in her late twenties and has had a number of love affairs - none of them satisfying physically or emotionally. She is plagued by guilt deriving from her parents' preference for a boy, and her lack of motherly guidance. She lives in Paris with her father, Colonel Anderson, whose job is to prepare for the contingency of invasion of France by the Commonwealth of Freedomloving Peoples [U.S.S.R.] by making evacuation plans for a French government in exile. The Colonel is perplexed by Europe's apparent lack of will to save itself from the tide of Communism. His relations with his daughter are cordial, though hampered by a lack of warm communication.

Julien Delattre is a writer, in his forties, whose burned cheek and limp derive from his service in the Spanish civil war in the thirties on the side of the Republican forces who were supported and eventually controlled by the Communist International. He had once written well-known poems on Communist themes, but he has since lost his Communist faith and now writes only occasional essays. He is a zealous anti-Communist and spends his time trying to rally intellectual and moral resistance to the growing Communist movement. Julien and his two friends, Boris and Professor Vardi, call themselves the Three Ravens Nevermore.

Professor Vardi is a former Communist from Eastern Europe. He, too, is anti-Communist, but he is also anti-anti-Communist. He has not cut off the ideological roots which made him a Communist in the first place.

Boris is also a refugee, from Poland. His wife and daughter were deported to Turkestan (in the Soviet Union) when the Communists took over Poland. Apparently, Boris was a middle-class farmer.

Leo Nikolayevitch Leontiev is a writer who has flourished under the Soviet Regime by compromising all his artistic principles for the sake of Communist success. He is a "Hero of Culture." But he has a good deal of difficulty writing because he does not really believe what he writes. His friend Gruber, who is engaged in research on psychological conditioning, told him that he could obtain peace of mind and the ability to write without nonartistic inhibitions by either seeking asylum on one of his many trips abroad or by permitting Gruber and his associates to brainwash him to the point where he believes what he writes under the aegis of Communism. But Leontiev refused to do either: he cannot seek asylum because his wife, Nina, is held hostage - not permitted to accompany Leontiev when he travels abroad on official "cultural" missions.

As the novel opens, it is Bastille Day [July 14, the anniversary of the onset of the French Revolution] and Hydie, her father, (Colonel Anderson), Fedya, Boris and several others are at a Bastille Day party given by Monsieur Anatole, a wealthy and aristocratic Frenchman who owns a publishing house. At seventy-five, Monsieur Anatole is still sharp, witty and perceptive. His gatherings are dominated by his learned, sarcastic and pessimistic monologues. His main **theme** is the destruction of the continuity of Western civilization as it fails to rise to its defense against the coming "Neanderthals," the Communists. Monsieur Anatole is cared for by his spinster daughter, Agnes, and his wastrel son, Gaston.

Hydie accidentally bumps Fedya and gives him a nosebleed. In taking off his jacket to wash he drops a notebook which Hydie, embarrassed by his gruff treatment of her, puts into her handbag. She leaves the party with Boris and is introduced to his two friends, Julien and Vardi, in a cafe. Hydie listens to the three discuss the effeteness of the West and the threat of Communism. Vardi still thinks in Communist categories and he has a certain animus for Boris, a "rightist." But Julien claims that categories of "right" and "left" no longer apply. What the West needs is a new faith to fill the vacuum left by the old, to give the West the identity and sense of purpose for which it longs. He, Hydie, and his friends are typical examples of the "faithless."

When Hydie is home alone she looks at Fedya Nikitin's notebook and sees lists of names with symbols beside them. Boris had said that Nikitin must be a member of the Soviet Secret Police, but Hydie does not believe that Nikitin is a spy. She goes to bed praying for something to believe in. The next day Hydie calls up Fedya to return his notebook. He is very relieved, for he feared punishment and exile because of his carelessness. He makes a date to take Hydie to the opera.

Julien Delattre meanwhile takes Hydie to a mass meeting of the Rally for Peace and Progress. There she is treated to the spectacle of Communists, fellow-travelers, and left-wing intellectuals shamelessly apologizing for the Soviet Union. Boris is among the pickets. Among the speakers are Professor Pontieux, a leading exponent of the philosophy of neo-nihilism - a philosophy which enables its adherents to justify any whim, including the claim that the Soviet Union is a great democracy. Another speaker is Lord Edwards, the famous English astronomer, who has compromised his scientific integrity in order to follow the Party Line about the nature of the universe. He is a Communist. Madame Tissier, a fellow-traveler and a writer, explains how her arrest by the Soviet Police on her most recent trip to the Soviet Union proves the absurdity of claims that the U.S.S.R. is a police state. It is merely watchful against its many enemies.

Emile Navarin, the French poet who is chairman of the meeting next introduces the featured speaker, Leontiev. Navarin is a Communist who has recently been rebuked by the Party and is eager to get back in its good graces. As Leontiev is about to read his prepared text, he is handed a note; whereupon he puts his text in his pocket and pulls out another one. Julien points out to Hydie that the Party Line has just been changed and that Leontiev had prepared two versions of his speech against just this possibility. Since Leontiev's speech is in praise of cultural diversity, Julien concludes that the U.S.S.R. has decided not to try to take over a small East European country - the "Rabbit State." Hydie seems attracted by the fact that these Communists and their supporters are possessed by a vital faith. She seems to prefer this to Julien's faithless cynicism. Fedya Nikitin is also seated on the speakers' platform at the Rally.

Instead of the Opera, Hydie and Fedya go to a cafe where they tell each other about their lives. Hydie self-consciously contrasts her unsatisfactory faithlessness with the psychological security of Fedya's Communist faith - which he calls the "scientific understanding of History." Hydie feels herself falling for Fedya.

The next day she visits Julien in his flat. Vardi is there. Julien remarks on the similarity between Hydie's guilt and longing after having lost her Christian faith and leaving the Church of Rome and that of Vardi and himself after having lost their Communist faith and leaving the Communist Party. He says that

Europe needs a new transcendental faith if it is to save itself from a new Dark Age. He explains to Hydie the reason he has stopped writing. He cannot tell the truth about the doom of European civilization: propaganda keeps breaking in, the urge to rally others to action - even though he knows that such action will not be forthcoming. Hydie leaves Julien and returns home with a craving for Fedya; she waits painfully for his call so that she can give herself to him.

Leontiev is to be the guest of honor at a soiree at Monsieur Anatole's. But before he goes he must prepare a version of the speech he gave at the Rally for Peace and Progress meeting to be cabled home [U.S.S.R.] for the next issue of the chief "cultural" publication. He is unable to work; he has been finding it increasingly difficult to write the Party Line that is expected of him. Suddenly, a half hour before the cable is due at the embassy, he is notified that his wife has been killed in an automobile crash. Fedya calls to offer his condolences and to tell him that he should nevertheless go to the affair at Monsieur Anatole's, since this is part of the cultural front in the war that the Free Commonwealth is waging against the West. After deciding to "go to Capua" - to seek asylum in the affluent West - Leontiev goes to Monsieur Anatole's.

The atmosphere at the gathering is one of excited relief, for the Free Commonwealth has decided only to demand certain extreme political and military concessions from the "Rabbit State" instead of swallowing it whole; the grave international crisis is over. All of the persons who were on the platform of the mass meeting of the Rally for Peace and Progress come to the soiree. In addition there is Father Millet, a Roman Catholic priest who tries to appeal to the modern temper and prejudice in his promotion of the cause of his church. With him is his niece, known for her promiscuity. Father Millet's protégé, the middle-aged novelist, Jean Dupremont, who writes pornographic novels with a Christian slant is also there. The conversation turns to the Fearless Sufferers, a small fanatical Christian sect in Leontiev's country, who practice many forms of physical and mental self-torture. Leontiev announces that he is in sympathy with this group, which is only trying to immunize itself against the terrible tyranny of the government. It is thus that Leontiev communicates to the gathering his apostasy from the Communist faith and his decision to stay in France. Professor Pontieux's wife, an actual Party member, turns on Leontiev bitterly. But Monsieur Anatole is delighted. A young American, Albert P. Jenkins, Jr., making an official study of American graveyards in Europe congratulates Leontiev. Leontiev is rebuked directly and vigorously by Lord Edwards for having changed sides after so many years, and, ambiguously, by Pontieux for aiding by his defection the forces of "reaction." In the course of the antiLeontiev harangue, Pontieux's wife, Matilda, beside herself with rage, admits that the left-wing neo-nihilist admirers and supporters of the Free Commonwealth are really convincing themselves that the inevitable domination of France by the Free Commonwealth is a most desirable event, so that they can manage to bear their subjugation. During the party Georges de St. Hilaire, a famous soldier of fortune who has gallantly fought all kinds of political oppression and who is violently anti-Communist, enters and delivers to Leontiev's ears a romantic monologue in praise of individual heroism. Late in the evening the French Communist poet, Navarin, comes in and announces that the "Father of the People" [No. 1, Stalin] has just died.

Interlude

Between the two parts of the novel, Koestler inserts a fantasy of contemporary international relations and the Cold War which serves to illustrate the weakness and vacillation of the West and the way it permits the Communists to snatch victory from defeat. The accidental detonation of an atomic bomb in the U.S.S.R. sets off a crisis which is resolved when the Free Commonwealth blames it on the "Rabbit State" and has a Communist government installed there.

AGE OF LONGING

TEXTUAL ANALYSIS

PART II

Professor Vardi, encouraged by the changes which follow the death of No. 1, accepts a post as professor of history at the University of Viennograd. Julien tries to talk him out of it, but it is useless. Vardi has never abandoned the Communist ideology. He was merely in opposition to the tyrannical reign of No. 1. It is not long, however, before Julien hears of the trial of Vardi for espionage. He has apparently become the victim of one of the periodic purges which mark every Communist country. Vardi and the others [no doubt, following the example of Rubashov] confess to having planned to poison the public water supply and are executed.

Worried about what he regards as the inevitable takeover by the Communists, Julien calls a meeting of prominent intellectuals at his flat for the purpose of discussing the formation of an "intellectual resistance movement" when France is "occupied." His guests include Boris, Touraine (the important newspaper editor), Dupremont, Father Mlllet, Leontiev, Plisson (a famous

Man of Letters) and Professor Pontieux (who broke with the Rally for Peace and Progress - the Communist Front - when the "Rabbit State" was taken over). But no one is interested in committing himself to anything concrete. After the editor and the Man of Letters have made their ambiguous comments and departed, Boris insults the ineffectual Pontieux who also leaves. Then Dupremont says that nothing can now be done and Leontiev suggests that only the way of the Fearless Sufferers is appropriate. Finally, when only Father Millet and Julien remain, Georges de St. Hilaire arrives late and makes his characteristic incisive and romantic speech implying that some reckless and violent act is the only thing appropriate to the problem. The failure of the meeting to resolve anything conclusively proves to Julien that all of France's capacity to resist the Communist tide has vanished.

Leontiev is given a contract by an American publisher to write his autobiography - emphasizing his break with the Free Commonwealth. But Leontiev has been compromising his artistic identity for more than two decades, and now that he has his chance to tell the truth, to ignore expediency, he is unable to write at all. Whatever talent he once had has apparently atrophied. He takes to drinking heavily and to frequenting the cafe Kronstadt - which is staffed mainly by exiles from Eastern Europe and the Free Commonwealth-persons who were in the second great wave of émigrés (after the Czarists), defectors from the Party, liberals, socialists and the like. To support himself Leontiev takes a job at the Kronstadt in which he recites poetry, mostly from the early days of the Revolution, dressed in the costume affected by Revolutionary leaders in those days. One night Fedya Nikitin and Hydie come to the Kronstadt. Fedya insults Leontiev by interrupting his act and then paying him off with a thousand-franc note. Leontiev has been plagued with guilt because of his failure to write; he dreams and then believes that Nina did not die an accidental death but rather sacrificed herself so that he could be free to write honestly. He accepts Fedya's tip, for he thinks he deserves such abasement; but then he throws a glass of champagne in Fedya's face. The next morning Leontiev is picked up by the French police to be extradited to the Free Commonwealth.

Hydie has now become Fedya's mistress. His attraction for her is at once physical and spiritual: his faith, his certainties, his Communism, give him a solidity that she and the other people she knows lack: this, in spite of Fedya's lack of warmth and real feeling for her. It is New Year's Eve in Fedya's apartment and the affair is several months old. In order to convince the disbelieving Hydie that people are just a bundle of conditioned reflexes that one can master and manipulate in the way Pavlov controlled the behavior of dogs, Fedya brings Hydie to a sexual **climax** with a quick caress under her left armpit. Stunned by his callous regard for human beings, Hydie breaks off their affair right there, and feels a good deal better for it.

The next day Hydie accompanies Julien on a visit to Boris who has been deteriorating rapidly in recent months in and out of hospitals and now lives in a dingy hotel room. They find him well on the way to insanity. He refuses to believe that the Father of the People is really dead and is determined to go to the Free Commonwealth for the purpose of assassinating him. To that end he is learning the art of becoming invisible. When Julien discovers that Hydie has broken off her affair with Fedya, he tells her that Fedya's real mission as "Cultural Attaché" of the embassy of the Free Commonwealth is to censor, collate and corroborate the various lists of potential resistors to the communization of the country which certain French Communists have the task of drawing up. The ultimate purpose is to "liquidate" this potential "resistance" when the Communists take over. There seems nothing that the French government can do about it. When the shocked Hydie relates the whole story to her father, he tells her that he did not want to interfere in her personal life before, even though her affair with Feyda had caused some concern in official circles and he had offered to resign.

Despite her father's and Julien's warnings she goes to the French Home Security Department and see Jules Commanche. Commanche is very like Julien, a former schoolmate. He points out that he is quite aware of the nature of Nikitin's work, but can do nothing about it. He goes on to discourse at length about the troubles of the age. France is aware of the fate that awaits it at the hands of the Free Commonwealth, but represses this knowledge because it is painful. The common people, deprived of their traditional religious faith, are fair game for Utopian mass movements. Only a new faith can meet the terrible challenge of the aggressive faith-movement [Communism]. The only thing that now remains to Frenchmen like St. Hilaire and Julien and Commanche is to die an heroic and gallant death. Hydie resolves to kill Nikitin in the hope that this dramatic gesture will force the public to focus its attention consciously on the sinister designs of Fedya and his government.

On the way upstairs to Fedya's apartment, Hydie meets Father Millet's niece coming downstairs: apparently, she is Fedya's new mistress. While she stands over him with her gun, Fedya, who has just admitted to himself that he has been a little corrupted by his association with Hydie and life in affluent France, tells her that she had the affair with him because of the power of his [Communist] faith in the future. He demonstrates his disdain for Western materialism by smashing the expensive radio of which he is so fond. Hydie forgets to release the safety catch and this gives Fedya a chance to lunge at her. She manages to shoot him on the second try. Then she runs out. However, she has only wounded Fedya in the groin and the Free Commonwealth Embassy and the French Government cooperate to hush things up. They treat the shooting as a lovers' quarrel. The Colonel resigns and takes a job in Washington. If she had been able to kill Nikitin, her plan to create a sensational public event and a trial for murder which would have brought her testimony to international attention might have succeeded. But now the only effect is the disgrace and demotion and recall to obscure duty of Fedya Gregoryevitch Nikitin.

It is now February, seven months after the opening of the novel in July. Monsieur Anatole is being buried and a procession of horse-drawn carriages follow the hearse. Public fear and panic are widespread because of rumors of an impending occupation of France by the armies of the Commonwealth of Peaceloving Peoples. There seems to be the possibility of atomic attack or of the arrival of clouds of atomic dust stemming from the explosions in the Commonwealth or of invasion by the Commonwealth Army. Hydie, her father and Jenkins are in one carriage. Commanche, who has resigned from the government, is in another with Georges de St. Hilaire. Commanche is going to join St. Hilaire's resistance movement - an armed band which the procession passes. Touraine and Plisson make up another party. Plisson nervously hopes that a false identity card will save him from "liquidation" when the occupation begins. Touraine is preparing to escape to Africa with his family. An unruly mob demonstrating on behalf of the Commonwealth clashes with the police. When Navarin says to Lord Edwards, his coach companion, that he would support the Free Commonwealth if France were invaded, Edwards comments disdainfully that that would be treason. Navarin is shocked by this sudden and unexpected and thoroughly English defection from the Party after so many years. Dupremont is riding with Mademoiselle Agnes who speaks of her happiness at being at last free of her father and implies that she is a member of an incipient French movement of the Fearless Sufferers. Julien and Father Millet pass the time discussing the great emptiness of the "age of longing." Julien considers Father Millet's faith as antiquated and false. He is unable to foresee the new faith which will replace the old. There remains, in the meanwhile, nothing to do except to make isolated retreats which will sustain temporarily some measure of humanity. The novel closes with Hydie meditating on the "age of longing."

AGE OF LONGING

GENERAL COMMENTARY

PHYSICAL STRUCTURE - PLOT

The plot of *The Age of Longing* is dominated by the affair of Hydie and Fedya. The novel then complicates the conventions of the romantic novel with political considerations. The other main plot lines are: Leontiev's break with the "Free Commonwealth" and his subsequent failure; Boris's decline into insanity as he fails to find any effective rational outlet for his opposition to Communism; Julien's meandering attempt to generate a resistance; Vardi's return to Communism; the approaching death of Monsieur Anatole. In the background of these relatively private stories looms the approaching specter of Communism. The Soviet Union's gathering momentum seems to promise either an outright occupation of France or the advent to power of the French Communist Party backed by the U.S.S.R. This "public" plot actually intrudes into and dominates the lives of all the characters, and occupies the "Interlude" between the two parts of the novel.

The novel is explicitly divided by the author into two parts (spaced by the "Interlude" given over to a fantasy of Cold War politics). The first part is a long and elaborate setting of the stage. The characters are brought together in the Paris of 19-; their histories are told. The second part sees the working out of the various sub-plots set in motion in the first half of the book. Monsieur Anatole's affairs, which bring most of the cast together at the beginning, middle, and end of the novel, serve as organizing and summarizing and unifying "centers."

Koestler never uses the term "Communism"; and he only mentions the U.S.S.R. once - to indicate that it has changed its name to the Commonwealth of Freedomloving Peoples. But there can be no doubt that Koestler is writing an historical novel about the Cold War and Communism.

THEMATIC STRUCTURE

Like all of Koestler's novels *The Age of Longing* is a novel of ideas. In Koestler's case, this means that he has an argument to make, a case to present. The novel's characters and their fortunes are thus illustrations of Koestler's thesis, his understanding of the "longing" of the twentieth century. Koestler wishes to reveal the form of individual and social existence in our time. He knows that the heart or essence of a society, a culture, a civilization, is a common faith - a concurrence of minds and wills on a myth or body of "truths" about God, man, society and the universe. This consensus of minds in a common faith not only makes social action possible and efficacious, it orders and pacifies individual lives. The central fact in the history of the last five hundred years of Western civilization is the decline, indeed the failure, of Christianity as the public faith, the accepted orthodoxy, which gives this civilization its substantial form. The novel attempts to be a revelation of the vacuum of social faith which renders Western society, especially Europe, brittle and weak and a prey for Communism.

Koestler sees the present time as a period of transition between two ages of faith: the dead Christian and the yet-to-be-born faith. He considers the political creed of egalitarianism engendered by the French Revolution as having proved its inadequacy to replace the transcendental faith of Christianity. That is why people are so ready to be taken in by demagogues preaching the Utopian promise of mass movements like Fascism and Communism. Whatever it turns out to be, the unknown future faith which will give meaning to individual and social life must be "religious" - that is, transcendental, offering to men a sense of their participation in a larger whole, giving them a purpose and a destiny which makes sense of life and death. Koestler has nothing specific to say about the content of this new social myth. We are living in an age of longing in which men's instincts cry out for some kind of transcendental fulfillment and as yet are answered only by emptiness or false prophets. Nevertheless, Julien Delattre, Koestler's voice in the novel, is confident that this next "mutation of consciousness" will someday occur.

The novel presents this analysis of contemporary Western civilization in the form of the biographies, reflections, conversations and actions of a number of representative persons. Although the action takes place in France, her weakness, fears and confusion represent all the other free Western countries. Although the United States is pictured favorably and as a powerful country, there is no indication that it possesses that public faith that alone can sustain the continuity of Western society.

THE ANATOMY OF CHARACTERS

The various characters are united by their self-conscious relationship to the central longing of the age - a faith to live by. There is really very little action in the novel, as there is very little plot. The motive for action is lacking in most of the cases. A haze of confusion engulfs the characters, even those who see most clearly. There is a hollowness at the center of their beings, of which they are all too conscious. Indeed, self-consciousness - that is, consciousness of the nature of the "problem" of Western society in this century - is the chief personal trait common to all the characters and a reflection of the characteristic that marks our age.

Since all the characters are very much aware of the historical situation they are caught in, they all render accurate expressions of Koetler's point of view. However, Julien and Commanche are the closest to Koestler's personal vision (these characters employ virtually the same language Koestler uses in a number of his political essays). And some of Hydie's reveries and the diary jottings of her father, Colonel Anderson, and Monsieur Anatole's reflections on the passing of French civilization are very close to the author's own thought. Georges de St. Hilaire is probably the character for whom Koestler has the greatest personal affection.

The cast of characters seems to represent a kind of anatomy of the self-conscious part of Western society. They understand each other quite well, because they are all responding to the same cultural problem. This is seen concretely in their various reactions to the specific threat of Communism and the Commonwealth of Freedomloving Peoples and in their different analyses of the malaise of the age. The responses range from the reaffirmation of traditional Christianity on one side to militant Communism on the other. Between these two alternatives lie variations of formlessness, including indifference, materialistic egoism, promiscuity, anti-Communism, superficial social engineering - basically motiveless and gratuitous gestures of protest against cruelty, self-deceiving explanations minimizing the depth of the crisis or misreading it as a new "freedom."

Father Millet represents the avant-garde of the Catholic Church, reaching out and trying to speak in the contemporary idiom of those alienated from the church. Koestler conceives of Christianity as outmoded, requiring too great a surrender of the critical faculties. He several times suggests that it is only a less dangerous form of the absolutism embodied in Communism. Father Millet, with his affectation of racy tolerance, seems as ineffectual as everyone else attending Julien's "emergency meeting" on intellectual resistance to the impending triumph of Communism in France.

Fedya Nikitin represents not only the inhuman terror that is Communism but also the power, self-confidence and aggressive success that comes from possessing a secure and comprehensive faith. Thus, Fedya cannot be stopped from fulfilling his mission as a member of the Secret Police, and the Communist Front groups flourish in France, and the "Free Commonwealth" succeeds in taking over other European countries. Julien is in love with Hydie, but Julien can offer her only a disillusionment more rationalized than her own. She finds Fedya attractive because his firm faith gives him a solid identity which manages temporarily to provide an ersatz fulfillment of her own longing for security. Koestler comments on the grotesque inhumanity of Communism by having Hydie discover with revulsion (in the brutal scene in his flat) that in Fedya's eyes she (and any human being) is no more than a material arrangement of "conditioned reflexes."

Hydie's own loss of her Christian faith is the second half of Koestler's explanation of the inadequacy of Christianity (Julien's declaration to Father Millet that Christianity involves the complete surrender of reason is the other half). She is unable to reconcile the action of a merciful God with the terrible suffering that goes on in the world He created. But in Hydie we see most clearly that it is - in her father's words - the "absence of God" that accounts for the present cultural crisis, that it is the "place of God" that must be filled. Koestler also indicates through the story of Hydie's convent experience what he considers to be the universal and permanent meaning of Christianity - a purely human pity for suffering humanity as symbolized through Christ's sacrifice on the cross.

The "Three Ravens Nevermore" represent three variants of an anti-Communist: the persecuted victim who fights back out of profound and helpless knowledge of what Communism really means (Boris); the ex-Communist who has never really given up the ideology and therefore can only oppose "Stalinism," not Communism (Vardi); the ex-Communist who has fully taken its measure and tries to make a serious and continual opposition to it (Julien). Boris's insanity renders him not only a casualty of Communism, but also ineffectual in his opposition to it. Vardi's case is typical of so many Western intellectuals who never get over their infatuation with the so-called "scientific understanding of History" that Communism pretends to be. Julien's inability to do anything really effective shows that the dimensions of the problem require more than conscious resistance, it requires a cultural transformation (the same could be said of the relative ineffectiveness of American material aid: send us a faith, Commanche says, instead of guns and bread). Julien also represents the dilemma of the contemporary writer, in which Koestler sees himself (as he tells us in *Arrow in the Blue*). The writer today stands midway between art and propaganda, between the artistic necessity to portray the truth about the end of the West and the psychological and ethical compulsion to urge one's comrades to action in order to defend it. The result in Julien's case is that he does not write; the result in Koestler's case (as he himself explains it) is that his novels tends to be "spoiled" by propaganda.

Two typical Americans are represented in the novel: the superficial "social engineer" and the well-meaning, but ineffective and confused though intelligent "liberal." Albert F. Jenkins, the young "researcher," approaches everything as a problem in statistics. Colonel Anderson, Hydie's father, see the significance of the age's longing, but is unable to do anything but note it in his diary. The inadequacy of his gentleman's code of secular liberalism is epitomized in his refusal to say anything to Hydie about Fedya's sinister mission on the grounds that he, her father, "has no right to interfere in her private life" (in spite of the fact that her affair might compromise her father, who holds a sensitive position, and her behavior is therefore by no means merely private).

Monsieur Anatole is in many ways the most interesting character in the book. Cynical, wealthy, aristocratic, egotistical and wise, the aged and dying publisher describes with precision the significance of the Cold War and the breakup of the West. His non-ideological love of "con-ti-nu-i-ty" is one of the chief landmarks in the intellectual landscape of the novel. The fact that Koestler chooses a decrepit figure who dies just as the occupation of France by the Communists seems most inevitable indicates he shortcomings of the substanceless notion of "continuity" - however civilized and superficially attractive it may be. The epicurean, flexible, tolerant culture which Monsieur Anatole represents can survive only on the capital of a genuine cultural faith which gives firmness and self-possession to a society.

There are three unsuccessful artists in the novel: Leontiev, Julien, and Dupremont. Julien's failure is explained above. Dupremont's consists in his attempt to use pornography in his novels in order to make a Christian message successful. His activity is also a Koestlerian comment on the degradation of Christianity. Leontiev's failure as a writer is twofold: he has compromised his artistic integrity by a quarter of a century of propagating the Party Line; when he finally is free to write honestly, he finds that he has nothing to say: his artistic ability has atrophied from dis- or mis-use.

The story of Arin (Fedya's Armenian grandfather) and Niko (his Georgian great-grandfather) introduces the nineteenth-century background of the disintegration of faith in the twentieth century. Both men are materialists (the "atom" is the basic reality), atheists and nationalists. The result of these nineteenth-century ideas is the Communism of the East and the religious sterility of the West.

There are two "places" in the novel which represent for Koestler provisional ideals - things that Koestler offers for want of the genuine article: the first is the romantic, violent, gallantry of Georges de St. Hilaire, who offers the gesture (without the faith) of a sincere crusader (Hydie steps for a moment onto the tragic plane on which St. Hilaire habitually moves, when she attempts to shock the world back to reality by assassinating Fedya); the second is the sect called the Fearless Sufferers, which represents an extreme attempt to develop a new ethic, a new myth, a new logic in order to cope with the barbarism of Communism against which other techniques have failed. These two alternatives are only ersatz modes of redemption in this age of longing. However much Koestler may admire the reckless, sacrificial daring of these two alternatives, he gives the last word to Julien who suggests that the only thing a sensitive man can do in this empty lost pause before the growth of a new and satisfying faith is to "build oases." Koestler evidently means some kind of refuge from the new barbarism where certain forms of the old life that give scope for proper human existence can still survive. This is not much; for though one might manage to obtain some comfort and avoid the worst excesses of the new barbarism, the longing will be yet unsatisfied, the "place of God" yet "vacant."

VIRTUES AND LIMITATIONS

The Age of Longing is another historical novel. It deals with the Cold War. But its merit consists in that it penetrates the issues which occupy the newspaper headlines to reveal the root malady of which the Cold War and the success of Communism are only the symptoms. That is why although the book was written from the relatively bleak Cold War perspective of 1950 and set in the (future) middle fifties, it is still of interest. The Cold War still goes on - though the West has a greater physical vigor than in the late forties. The Communist threat, though it has changed its guise somewhat, is still worldwide. Koestler's analysis of what is really the radical need of our society - namely, a true civilizational faith - is as pertinent as ever. His rendering of Communist faith in the person of Fedya will still be a revelation to most persons who read the book. And the portrait of French Communist intellectuals and of fellow-travelers is authentic satire.

It is likely that many of the characters in the book are modeled on actual persons. Some readers might see the figure of Merleau Ponty in the fellow-traveling "neo-nihilist" Professor Pontieux. It seems likely that Georges de St. Hilaire is modeled after Richard Hillary, the young English writer and fighter pilot who fought gallantly in the air war over Britain and died in 1943. (See the essay on Hillary in *The Yogi and the Commissar*.) There are probably living models of Lord Edwards, the British scientist and Communist, and of Navarin, the French poet-Communist. The philosophy of "neo-nihilism" is undoubtedly a

parody of French existentialism which claims to be a philosophy of freedom and is used by many of its exponents - especially, its progenitor, Sartre - to justify Communism and the policy of the U.S.S.R.

Koestler has made his central point - the age is longing for a faith - dramatically clear and convincing. The conversations - intellectual and abstract as they are - are always brilliantly compelling. Some of the scenes are staged with a director's sure sense of melodrama, especially Monsieur Anatole's three gatherings and the mass meeting of the Rally for Peace and Progress. *The Age of Longing* deserves a place beside Constantine Fitzgibbon's *When the Kissing Had to Stop* as one of the most successful of contemporary political fables.

Yet, although the reader will have enjoyed the novel and will have been the wiser for having read it, he is likely to be disappointed in its outcome. The second half of the novel does not live up to the brilliant promise of its beginning. Part of the reason for this is Koestler's own interpretation of his subject. He is very much in the position of Julien Delattre, knowing all the questions, but none of the important answers. The age of longing does not have the answer which the age requires, so the second half of the book is bound to disappoint; it disappoints the characters as well as the reader.

The novel, Koestler would say was written to show the age of longing, which is a time of longing for faith without the satisfaction of finding it. The book merely mirrors the emptiness and disappointment of the age. But this explanation does not adequately account for the let-down one experiences in the novel; it is not so much its subject as its form that dictates the brittleness and superficiality of much of the novel. As a novel of ideas the characters are accorded a secondary interest. Although there is a brilliant and interesting cast, once introduced they are given no significant development, no significant personal fulfillment. The conversations and discussions are not dynamic encounters which either progressively reveal an individual human nature or show that human nature working its way to a destiny. To be sure, there is a developing self-revelation in the Leontiev sub-plot, and there is a "logical" change in Boris's experience. The former case is of the highest interest, but Koestler did not lavish the space and attention on it that would have transformed Leontiev's story into the profound tragedy it could easily have been. Leontiev is on the periphery of the novel; he is not directly touched by the ideas which govern the talk and action of Julien and Hydie and Fedya. Had Koestler approached Leontiev as he did the character of Rubashov, and spent on him the same kind of painstaking effort to show the pathos of his moving mind, Leontiev would have taken his place with Rubashov as one of the fictional tragic figures of the age. As it is, Leontiev's story, the revelation of the hulk the man's life of lies has made of him, is treated mechanically and quickly; we see only the result, not the moral freedom of his past fatal decision to sell himself; for Koestler's main interest lies elsewhere.

But the ideas which govern the presentation of Hydie and Julien, do not really enter their lives as character - changing experiences. In a sense, there are no problems for them. There is nothing for them to resolve because there is nothing they can resolve. Hydie only has to discover the true nature of Communism, something of which she has been almost willfully ignorant. But Communism never enters her consciousness as a challenge or a temptation with which she must deal. Thus, nothing really happens to Julien and Hydie; they are illustrations of spiritual emptiness and futility. They serve Koestler's purposes admirably, but they do not offer the reader the kind of dynamic human drama he has come to expect from novels. In *The Brothers Karamazov*, the brothers Ivan, Dmitry and Alyosha must deal with the "ideas" in their own lives. They debate them with each other and themselves. They must make profound resolutions, profound decisions; they must determine their spiritual destinies as they simultaneously reflect on the arguments. A great deal happens in the individual lives of the three brothers as they think and act, therefore discovering what it is to be human. The absence of dynamic action (the dramatization of moral success and failure) in the lives of his characters makes Koestler's *Age of Longing* a comprehensive and intelligent parable for which his characters are merely illustrations.

But if the form of Koestler's novel makes his characters of limited interest as human beings, the level of his ideas and the adequacy of his treatment of his subject renders the book somewhat superficial even as a novel of ideas. For example, Communism is the only secular ideology presented in the novel. But in the non-Communist West other ideologies are important forms of thought and action. Koestler has no place in his book for progressivism or democratism. Although he may have considered these no match for Communism, they do determine the patterns of thought of many who govern and influence Western societies. And whatever one thinks of Koestler's opinion of Christianity, he hardly gives it a vigorous champion in the person of Father Millet. The Christian Dostoevsky gave the atheists a much greater range of argument and dramatic action in his novels.

Though Koestler's proposition that the question of faith is the great one of our age is undoubtedly right and saves the novel from triviality, he is unable to develop this question into a satisfying exploration of human nature and history. His philosophy, beyond this central shrewd observation, is practically nonexistent. One comes away from *The Age of Longing* with the satisfaction of having read an entertaining, amusing and instructive account of the confusion of the time. But one does not come away with a deepened knowledge of human psychology, of human nature, nor with a better understanding of man's existence in history. Koestler has reached the limits of his philosophy, and has no further answers.

The serious limitations of form and subject that Koestler imposed on himself are well illustrated by his treatment of Hydie. Much of the novel is given over to the story of her love affair with Fedya. As soon as she understands the brutality of the ideology he serves, she realizes that he is an ersatz and unworthy comfort for her longing for faith. Koestler relegates the story of her past religious experiences, the gradations, variations and development of her religious life, as well as her loss of faith and her marriage, to a summary chapter and a summary conversation. But the story of her past excites the reader's interest whenever it appears. That it is only partly represented indicates Koestler's reluctance to explore dramatically, debate and elaborate (say, in something of the manner he used in Rubashov's case) the issues raised by Hydie's story - before and during her loss of faith. He might have also explored, analogously, Julien's possession and loss of his Communist faith. Because Koestler puts these fascinating stories in the background of the book (in the past, rather than in the present), because he wants instead to focus on the Paris scene and the ineffectual resistance to Communism, he cheats the reader of a full revelation of how he has come to his conclusion about the age of longing. He skips over the crucial stages in the crumbling of the social psyche of Western society (as illustrated in Hydie's past), and the result is a contemporary fable that is merely excellent "journalism."

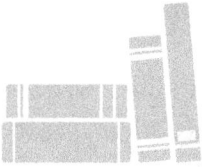

AGE OF LONGING

CRITICAL COMMENTARY

Critics have paid little attention to Koestler for four reasons. First, many pro-Communists can have nothing but hostility for his work. Even many non-Communists find his aggressive attack on Communism and its works distasteful. Second, as Koestler himself notes in *The Invisible Writing*, "political" and topical novels are not considered by many critics who snobbishly ignore works outside the range of their experience. Third, Koestler is not mainly a novelist. His five novels make up less than a third of his published books. He can hardly be said to have devoted his life to writing novels. Fourth, only one of these novels, *Darkness at Noon*, is an undoubted masterpiece.

One can dismiss outright the self-serving criticism of Communists and pro-Communists. It has neither a sincere literary basis nor any appeal to those who do not adhere to this ideology. But beyond these outright pro-Communist writers, there are a good number of persons who are made uncomfortable by Koestler's books because they cannot sympathize with genuine, frank and active hostility to Communism and the Soviet Union. These "progressives" call Koestler's writings "reactionary." Typical of this kind of criticism is John Strachey's chapter on four anti-Communist writers in *The Strangled Cry*. He finds Koestler's *Darkness at Noon* excessively anti-rationalist. "There is something hysterical...about *Darkness at Noon*... The literature of reaction has done its work... The catastrophe of Communist rationalism must not make us despair of reason... It is also a reaction against five hundred years of rationalism and empiricism." This is what disturbs critics like Strachey. Koestler's critique of Communism goes to its rationalist roots; it therefore implies a similar critique of other forms of extreme rationalism; and rationalism in its political forms is well entrenched in contemporary Western society. Socialists like Strachey and those who appear to write from a Marxist bias like the very useful English critic Arnold Kettle (*Introduction to the English Novel*, Vol. II) disagree with Koestler's critique of reason, and therefore find the novels politically and philosophically unfruitful.

The best of Koestler's "political" critics is George Orwell. In his essay on Arthur Koestler he finds Darkness a Noon to have the stature of high tragedy. Better than anyone else he has described what Koestler is doing in his novels: Koestler is "trying to write contemporary history, but unofficial history, the kind that is ignored in the textbooks and lied about in the newspapers." And it is as contemporary history that people will continue to read Koestler's novels and the four volumes of his autobiography. This interest suffices even when the novels do not attain the human interest and artistic perfection of *Darkness at Noon*.

Orwell has also put his finger on another problem that Koestler's books pose for critics: "None of them escapes for more than a few pages from the atmosphere of nightmare." In *The Invisible Writing* Koestler comments on the refusal of English critics to believe that the melodrama of his novels is based on the terrible melodrama of contemporary history which they, unlike Koestler, have not experienced directly. Representative of those critics who are repelled by the absence of what they call "normality" in Koestler's novels is Raymond Mortimer. "He accepts as normal what I believe and hope is abnormal." Yet even Mr. Mortimer calls Thieves in the Night "a masterpiece of propaganda," and he adds, "[There are] few who write about the diseases of our civilization with anything approaching his acuteness and fervor."

Other critics, in a more literary vein, tend to agree that, in the words of V. S. Pritchett, Koestler is "unable to create and sustain a large character." Rubashov is generally excepted from this criticism. And the vividness of his realized consciousness is sufficient to make the other characters in the novel acceptable. But Koestler's lack of interest in creating characters who engage us for their own sake, instead of merely dramatizing historical problems, keeps his novels (again with the exception of *Darkness at Noon*), according to Pritchett, merely at the level of superb reportage. Pritchett commends Koestler for his ability to handle argument "in a living way." But he sees Koestler's writing as "melodramatic" and "theatrical," full of theatrical "generalizations, simplifications." *Darkness at Noon*, Pritchett says, is a "tour de force." "When all praise is given, *Darkness at Noon* remains a melodrama...powerful, but not an imaginative work of the highest kind.... [Koestler's books] are not novels: they are reports, documentaries, briefs, clinical statements." Pritchett considers *The Gladiators* Koestler's best book.

Thus, most critics concur in Peter Viereck's estimate that Koestler's *Darkness at Noon* is a permanent masterpiece and the rest of his novels are of "journalistic" interest, though some have high praise for *The Gladiators*. Koestler himself seems to agree. In *The Arrow in the Blue* he confesses that he has "spoiled most of [his] novels out of a sense of duty to some cause; [he] knew that the artist should not exhort and preach, and [he] kept on exhorting and preaching." In *The Invisible Writing* he refers to "the topical dross which tends to clutter up [his] other books" [other than *The Gladiators*]. (See also Koestler's essay "The Novelist's Temptations" in *The Yogi and the Commissar*.)

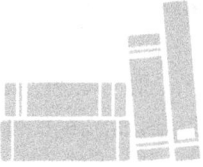

AGE OF LONGING

ESSAY QUESTIONS AND ANSWERS

....

Question: Why is Leo Nikolayevich Leontiev unable to write the "one honest book of his life"?

Answer: Leontiev had been a "Hero of Culture," writing "works of art" on cue. Now, defected from the Free Commonwealth, he is finally able to write as he longs to. For twenty years he had been convinced that, given the opportunity to escape, all he would have to do would be to "…open the sluices and all the material… would pour out like a torrent." He had already written whole chapters of the book in his head, but he had never put anything on paper, for he felt that it would be much harder for him to go on functioning as a Hero of Culture if he did.

Leontiev had always been able to work on command under the most severe and degrading pressure. Now on his own the words are dried up; he finds that he cannot even function by accepting his agent's suggestion and, using a crisp, dramatic style, write about the more sensational aspects of the system he fled from. Leontiev, loathing himself, cries that this isn't his "style," but "…the style in which he had been writing for the past twenty years was not his style either. At some point during that long, dreary journey he had lost his identity."

Leontiev's is the fate of a man who has compromised with evil, losing his soul in the process. He began by abhorring the system which held him captive. He told himself he would have to work along with it, but only because this was necessary for his survival; he did not sanction any of it and would create according to his own values when he was free. But his work very successfully advanced the cause he loathed and it became more difficult for him to rationalize his action. He stopped thinking about what he was doing to lessen the discomfort. Thus, by aiding what he despised he was destroying his own values.

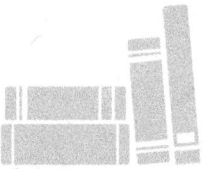

BIBLIOGRAPHY

NOVELS

The Gladiators. London, 1939.

Darkness at Noon. New York, 1941. Signet paperback edition, New York, 1962. This edition contains a helpful introduction by Peter Viereck.

Arrival and Departure. New York, 1943.

Thieves in the Night. New York, 1946.

The Age of Longing. New York, 1951. Collier paperback edition, New York, 1962.

AUTOBIOGRAPHY

Dialogue with Death. New York, 1955. (First published, 1938.) Macmillan paperback edition, New York, 1960.

Scum of the Earth. New York, 1955. (First published 1941.)

Arrow in the Blue. New York, 1952. Macmillan paperback, New York, 1961.

The Invisible Writing. New York, 1954. Beacon paperback, Boston, 1955.

The God That Failed, ed. Richard Crossman. New York, 1950. Bantam paperback edition, New York, 1959. Six authors tell of their infatuation with Communism and subsequent disenchantment (Koestler, Silone, Richard Wright - ex-Communists; Gide, Louis Fischer, Stephen Spender - ex-fellow-travelers).

ESSAYS

The Yogi and the Commissar. New York, 1945. Collier paperback edition, New York, 1945.

Promise and Fulfillment. New York, 1950.

The Trail of the Dinosaur. New York, 1955.

Reflections on Hanging. New York, 1957.

The Lotus and the Robot. New York, 1961.

Suicide of a Nation, ed. Arthur Koestler. London, 1963.

THEATRE

Twilight Bar. London, 1945.

SCIENCE

Insight and Outlook. New York, 1950. Univ. of Nebraska paperback edition, 1965.

The Sleepwalkers. New York, 1959. Universal Library paperback edition, New York, 1963.

The Act of Creation. New York, 1964.

CRITICISM

Atkins, John A. *Arthur Koestler.* New York, 1956. The only available full-length study of Koestler. Covers the period down to 1955. A helpful study, though it is very personal and mostly superficial. It deals primarily with Koestler's political thinking. The chapter on *Darkness at Noon* is good.

Beum, Robert. "Epigraphs for Rubashov," *Dalhousie Revue*, XLII (1962), pp. 86-91. Sound comments on *Darkness at Noon* as tragedy and a fair discussion of the epigraphs Koestler used to head each section of the book.

Mortimer, Raymond. "The Art of Arthur Koestler," *The Cornhill*, Nov. 1946, pp. 212-222. Some shrewd criticism of Koestler's novels. A good example of what many English critics have to say against Koestler's novels.

Orwell, George. "Arthur Koestler," *Collected Essays.* London, 1961. Written in 1944, Orwell's essay presents interesting political insight into Koestler.

Padev, Michael. "The Autobiography of Arth*r K**stl*r," *Punch*, XVII (1954), pp. 149-151. A **parody** of Koestler's frequently annoying flaunting of his "guilt complex" in his autobiography.

Pritchett, V. S. "Arthur Koestler," *Horizon*, XV (1947), pp. 233-47. (Also included in *Books in General.* New York, 1953.) The best presentation available on Koestler's virtues and limitations as a writer of fiction, though Pritchett does not deal much with *Darkness at Noon*.

Stace, Walter. *The Teachings of the Mystics*. Mentor paperback edition, New York, 1960. Discusses Koestler's "mystical experience" in prison in Spain.

Strachey, John. *The Strangled Cry*. New York, 1962. A good example of the revulsion Koestler's critique of Communism and extreme rationalism provokes in many leftist intellectuals.

Viereck, Peter. "Forward" to the Signet paperback edition of *Darkness at Noon*. A sensitive and very informative introduction to Koestler's masterpiece.

BACKGROUND (ESPECIALLY FOR DARKNESS AT NOON)

Koestler's essays collected in *The Yogi and the Commissar* and *The Trail of the Dinosaur* and his autobiography (*Arrow in the Blue* and *The Invisible Writing*) discuss the **themes** and problems found also in his novels. The first essay in *The Yogi and the Commissar* is especially relevant to *Darkness at Noon*, and there is an illuminating chapter on this novel in *The Invisible Writing*.

Bochenski, J. M. and Niemeyer, G., ed. *Handbook on Communism*. New York, 1963. An invaluable one-volume reference book.

Chambers, Whittaker. *Witness*. New York, 1952. A sensitive and revealing autobiography by an American ex-Communist who spied for the Soviet Union. This book makes an interesting American complement to Koestler's European account of the twenties and thirties. The introduction is a penetrating analysis of Communist faith.

Grossman, Richard, ed. *The God that Failed*. New York 1950. Bantam paperback edition, New York, 1959. Koestler and five others discuss the Communist faith.

Kingsley, Sidney. *Darkness at Noon*. New York, 1951. An adaptation for the stage.

Meyer, Frank S. *The Moulding of Communists*. New York, 1961. The standard scholarly study of the Communist mind.

Krivitsky, Walter. *I Spied for Stalin*. New York, 1939. General Krivitsky, ex-chief of Soviet intelligence in Europe (and later murdered by Stalin's agents), gives an authoritative confirmation of Koestler's "theory of confession."

Sperber, Manes, *The Burned Bramble*. New York, 1951. A masterly revelation of the Communist mind in a novel by an ex-Communist who worked with Koestler in Paris.

Serge, Victor. *The Case of Comrade Tulayev*. Anchor paperback edition, New York, 1963. One of the best novels on Communism.

Weissberg, Alexander. *Conspiracy of Silence*. London, 1952. The experience of Eva Weissberg in Soviet prisons was used by Arthur Koestler in writing *Darkness at Noon*.

www.ingramcontent.com/pod-product-compliance
Lightning Source LLC
LaVergne TN
LVHW011710060526
838200LV00051B/2833